Coaches, Carriages, and Carts

TYPE, USE, DESIGN, AND INDUSTRY

BROUGHT TO YOU BY

The books created by Equine Heritage Institute are designed to preserve the history and majesty of the horse. Our goal is to find, understand, and pass on the valuable data about equine use and its influence on humanity. The Equine Heritage Institute is a not for profit 503(c) and 100% of all proceeds from the sale of books, services, and products support Equine Heritage Institute's mission.

To make a donation to EHI, please visit www.ehi-donations.com

The Horse

"We have had 6,000 years of history with the domesticated horse and only 100 years with the automobile."

Gloria Austin

MEET OUR EHI TEAM

Abby David, Graphic Designer

Abby David's family has roots in the Walking Horse tradition and she grew up hearing tales of Ole Tobe the mule's antics, holiday wagon decorations, and trick riding. In her teens she spent her summers boarding the neighbors horses and playing at barrel racing in the back paddock with Thunder. She landed a job as a Graphic Designer at The Arts Center of Cannon County in 2004 and has worked in the print and digital mass communications industry continuously. Since marrying into a family in the racehorse business, she has enjoyed exploring a whole new world of horses and wearing big fancy hats. She also enjoys dancing in all it's forms and teaches Modern Folkloric styles her local community.

Gloria Austin's Collection of Books

www.GloriaAustin.com

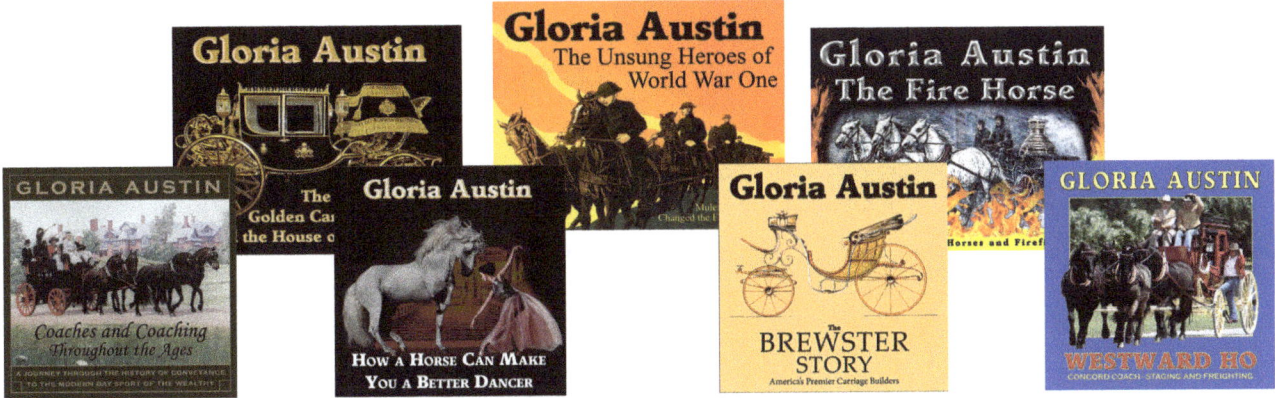

ENJOY OUR OTHER BOOKS

- How a Horse Can Make You a Better Dancer
- The Brewster Story
- Carriage Lamps
- Gloria Austin's Carriage Collection
- A Glossary of Harness Parts
- Equine Elegance
- The Fire Horse
- Horse Basics 101
- The Unsung Heros of World War One
- The Horse, History, and Human Culture
- Horse Symbolism
- Horses of the Americas
- A Drive Through Time: Carriages, Horses, and History
- Speak Your Horse's Language
- Tea: Steeped in Tradition
- The Golden Carriage and the House of Hapsburg
- Coaches and Coaching Throughout the Ages
- Westward Ho
- The Medieval Horse
- Womena and Horses

Brought To You By The Equine Heritage Institute

Coaches, Carriages, and Carts
By: Gloria Austin, President of Equine Heritage Institute, Inc. (EHI)

First Publish Date 2020
Copyright © 2020 by Equine Heritage Institute, Inc.

All rights reserved. No part of this publication may be reproduced, distributed, or transmitted in any form or by any means, including photocopying, recording, or other electronic or mechanical methods, without the prior written permission of the publisher, except in the case of brief quotations embodied in critical reviews and certain other noncommercial uses permitted by copyright law. For permission requests, write to the publisher, addressed "Attention: Permissions Coordinator," at the address below.

Gloria Austin Carriage Collection, LLC; Equine Heritage Institute, Inc.
3024 Marion County Road Weirsdale, FL 32195 Office: (352) 753-2826 Fax: (352) 753-6186

Ordering Information:
Quantity sales: Special discounts are available on quantity purchases by corporations, associations, and others. For details, contact the publisher at the address above.
Printed in the United States of America First Edition
ISBN: 978-1-951895-00-6 Print, 978-1-951895-01-3 E-book

Table of Contents

Acknowledgements 6
Foreword 7
How to Identify a Horse Drawn Carriage 8
    The Axel 10
    Springs 12
    The C-Spring 14
    The Wheel 16
    Forecarriage 18
    Two-Wheel Vehicles 20
    Carriage Tops 24
    Carriage Lamps 26
    The Breaks 28
The Phaeton Family 30
The Jenny Lind 32
The Curricle 34
The Hansom Cab 36
Park Drag 38
Road Coach 40
The Chariot 42
The Dress Chariot 44
The Coat of Arms 46
The Royal Mail Coach 48
Evolution of the American Coach Body 50
    The Concord Coach 52
    The American Sleigh 56
    The Mitchell 58
    Trotting Racing 60
The Kladruber 62
The Morgan 64
The Bridle 66
The Driving Bit 68
The Bearing Rein 70
Evolution of the Harness 72
    The Harness 1 74
    The Harness 2 75
    Pair Harness 2 Full Collar 76
    Pair Harness 3 Breast Collar 77
Driving 78
    National Reining Styles 80
Whips 82
Signals 83
Tandem 84
Postilion Driving 86
Coaching and the Four-in-Hand 88
The Ladies Four-in-Hand Driving Club 90
Livery 92
Glossary 94

COACHES, CARRIAGES, AND CARTS: TYPE, USE, DESIGN, AND INDUSTRY

ACKNOWLEDGMENTS

Thank you to Kenneth Wheeling, who created the
original education boards this book is based on.

Kenneth Wheeling holds a degree in classical languages (Greek and Latin) from St. Bonaventure University and a master's degree in education from St. Michael's College in Vermont. Ken is associate editor of The Carriage Journal and a widely published author of articles and books on horse-drawn vehicles. With Richard C. V. Nicoll, he is co-chair of the Carriage Association of America International Carriage Symposium.

Photo by Linda Freeman

SPECIAL THANKS TO THE CARRIAGE ASSOCIATION OF AMERICA

The Carriage Association of America (CAA) was founded in 1960 and is the oldest and largest international organization devoted to the preservation and restoration of animal-drawn carriages and sleighs. To enjoy the pleasure of collecting, driving, or learning about carriages with others, contact this membership organization through the following website: www.caaonline.com

The Carriage
Association of America
3915 Jay Trump Rd.
Lexington, KY 40511
859-231-0971
info@caaonline.com

CAA Driver Proficiency Program
Participation in this program will help to increase your awareness and knowledge of driving, how to do so safely and correctly, and earn you a CAA Driver Proficiency Certificate.

In addition to evaluating drivers' proficiency at the various levels, this program allows for those interested in becoming driving instructors to accomplish the prerequisites at the stages of Level 1, Level 2, Level 3, Evaluators, and Instructors. This will ensure the standard for traditional driving and horsemanship skills will continue.

Foreword
by Gloria Austin

There was a time when "cut and paste" was the way to create what I called Education Boards in the Gloria Austin Carriage Museum. Foam boards (24"x36") on easels were spread throughout the 40,000 square foot museum for the public to learn about carriages, horses, and the people who tended and drove them for transportation in a bygone era.

As my Library and Museum were being formalized, Kenneth Wheeling came to Florida one winter and copied and pasted information that I thought important for Museum guests. He was a charm with whom to work since he knew the terminology of the horse-drawn carriage and its history in American and European tradition. Pictures, even if black and white, are "worth a thousand words." And, in the process of illustration, pictures also made the text more believable.

Many white folding tables were used to spread magazines and books atop. There was a copier sitting in the corner that could enlarge the images and text. Cut to size on white paper images were glued onto almost 48 foam boards. The paper started to curl so eventually we had to put a light film covering over the boards.

Not only did the guests at the Museum learn from these education boards, so did the docents or volunteers who acted as greeters and guides in the Museum. Linda Beaulieu, who organized the Library and originally trained docents, was helpful in conveying Education Board information. Dick Magnum formalized this information into a three-ring binder that served as a Docent Training Manuel. In addition, docents and guests learned from individual placards in front of each of 184 carriages. Volunteers and guests gathered insights into this bygone era from streaming Power Point presentations, lifestyle charts, and special displays depicting the time before the automobile, before refrigeration, and before modern communication. I also gave two-hour lectures on Mondays which gave trainees an opportunity to learn about carriages and my travels with horses at driving competitions in the United States, Canada, and Europe.

We are now working in a more modern medium. InDesign has allowed Abby David to take the scanned education boards and turn them into this book, which I hope you share with friends. It portrays a time when horses were put to Coaches, Carriages, and Carts. You will learn about the types, use, and design of carriages. You can also order and read any of my over 20 books to enjoy the skill and knowledge of the people and horses who moved America into modernity.

HOW TO IDENTIFY A HORSE DRAWN VEHICLE

Horse-drawn vehicles are the foundation of modern transportation. These vehicles produced many innovations used today. Other than observing a horse pull a carriage, there are proper ways to identify these vehicles and their unique characteristics.

A horse-drawn vehicle is composed of two major parts. There is the **body** where the driver and passengers ride. Then there is the **gear**, which is the combination of wheels, axle, reach and springs making a mechanical cradle for the body. The name of a carriage is generally determined by the style of its body. For example, the carriage featured here is a *Stick-Seat, Coal Box Buggy*. The buggy's name comes from the shape of its rear, being curved to resemble a coal scuttle.

A carriage body consists of several components, all of which have proper names and identified as such by the carriage maker. Basic carriage appointments can include as follows:

- DASHBOARD
- TOEBOARD
- SILL
- SEAT RISER
- SEAT
- SEAT CUSHION
- FOLDING TOP
- GROOM'S SEAT
- STEP PLATE
- SKIRT
- RAIL
- REMOVEABLE LAMPS
- TOP

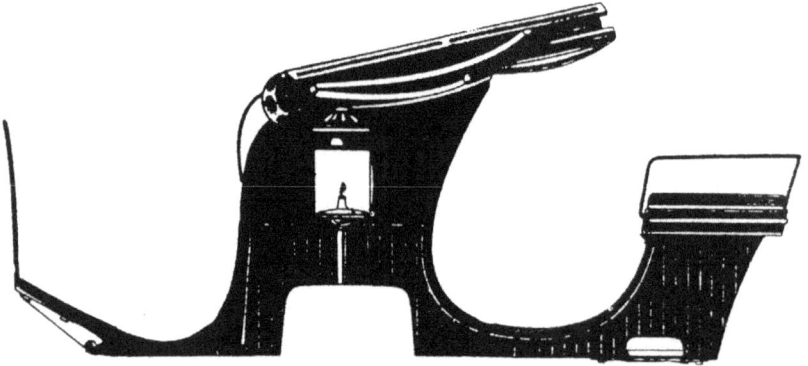

8 COACHES, CARRIAGES, AND CARTS: TYPE, USE, DESIGN, AND INDUSTRY

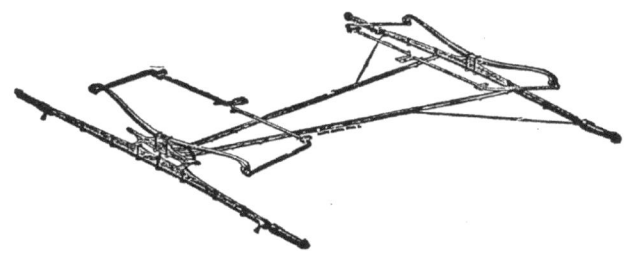

Some of the more popular style of carriages include:

-Brougham	-Landau
-Victoria	-Roof-seat Break
-Stanhope Phaeton	-Rockaway
-Side-bar Runabout	-Wagonette Break

The gear at the above has two axles, a set of Mulholland Springs (Cray Bros., Cleveland, Ohio), a double reach, and a fifth wheel assembly. The fifth wheel is the mechanism at the center of the front axle which permits the axle to turn. The development of the articulating front axle took three thousand years. The distance the axle can turn is called the **lock.**

Carriage wheels were made by **Wheelwrights**, a person who makes or repairs wooden wheels. They had constructed wheels with the mechanical features of a dish and camber. It was their job to fit together the three major components of a wheel: Hub, Spoke, and Felloe. The tire was applied later on to protect the felloes from road damage. The development of the wheel embodies the whole development of an animal-powered vehicle. Now taken for granted, it is one of man's greatest inventions.

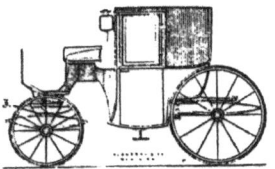
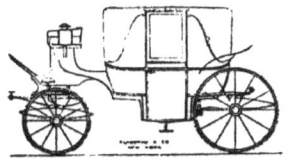
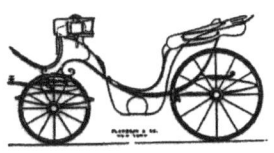

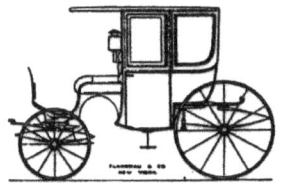

COACHES, CARRIAGES, AND CARTS: TYPE, USE, DESIGN, AND INDUSTRY

The Axle

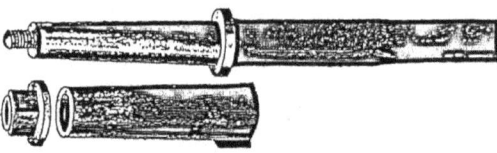

No matter the size, axles needed lubrication in order to allow the wheel to turn freely. If the metal boxing turns upon a metal axle, without the benefit of lubricant, the wheel would seize up, i.e. the metal parts would heat up and fuse together.

THE MAIL AXLE

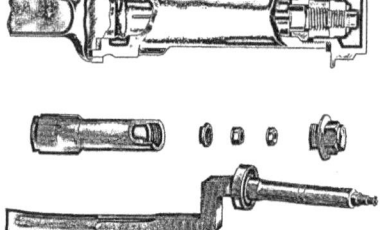

One of the major types of improvements was the invention of the axle, which used oil, rather than grease as a lubricant. In 1786, John Besant patented a new wheel carriage, which included a new type of axle. It created a chamber in which oil could be stored. The wheel was held on the axle by a moon plate, a metal plate surrounding the axle, using three bolts, which pierced the hub of the wheel. It was sealed with a leather washer to keep the oil from leaking out. Since this type of axle was extensively used on Mail Coaches, it was called the **Mail Axle.**

The **axle** is the most basic component of a carriage. It holds the wheels. Experiments and patents for different kinds of axles proliferated during the time of carriage makers. The first improvements were metal plates, attached to the ends of the plain and wooden axle. Gradually, iron and then steel axles came to be the standard type of axle used in carriage construction. The **steel axle** consists of a steel bar, whose ends have been fashioned into a spindle. The end is turned further down and threaded to accommodate a nut. A collar is fitted behind the spindle to stop the wheel from going further.

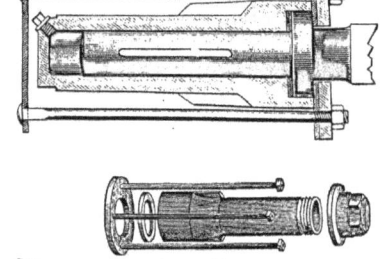

A metal boxing was fitted inside the wooden hub of the wheel, which permitted the wheel to rotate. This was a simple axle.

THE COLLINGE AXLE

Referred to as the Patent Axle, the axle invented by coach maker, John Collinge in 1792, became the most accepted axle for heavy type carriages. The boxing of the wheel fitted against a collar on the axle. The wheel was held on by a series of metal fittings, all of which had to be put on in proper sequence. The innermost piece was a brass collet, which had a flat top. This was followed by two nuts which had opposite threads. The whole was secured by a cotter pin, and an oil cap filled with oil was then screwed onto the boxing with inside threads.

PORTER PATENT DUST PROOF AXLE....

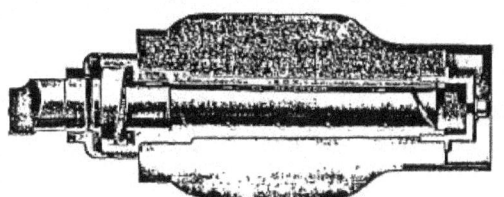
DOLSON'S SELF-OILING AXLE

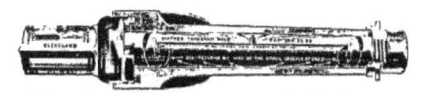
The Mather "Thousand Mile" Axle

THIS IS THE
Richards "Long Distance" Axle.

Brewer Longitudinal
AXLE LUBRICATOR.
Will Run 3 to 6 Months with One Oiling.

Since there were many lighter varieties of carriages, attention was constantly paid to improving the axles used on them. Hundreds of patents were granted for every minuscule improvement. The Mather "Thousand Mile" Axle was patented in 1899, in Cleveland, Ohio. The Richards "Long Distance" Axle was a product of the Sheldon Axle Company (Wilkes Barre, PA), probably the largest axle maker in America. The Porter Dust-proof (1899) and the Brewer Axle (1885) were both attempts at trying to lessen the number of times one had to grease the axle. They had grooves in the axles which acted as a reservoir for additional grease.

FAQ FOR THE CARRIAGE OWNER:
One of the most commonly asked questions is what kind of grease should I use? Here are some things to consider when making this choice:

- Ordinary grease axles should be greased with all-purpose bearing grease.
- Oil axles, which have grooves fitted with felt pads to hold the oil, require an SAE. 90 gear oil.
- Oil axles, such as the Mail Axle or the Collinge Axle, require S.A.E 30 (or 40). A high-grade oil containing molybdenum can also be used.

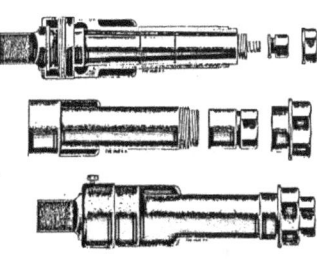
IT IS ABSOLUTELY IMPOSSIBLE FOR A GREASE CAP TO COME OFF OR WORK LOOSE WITH THIS ATTACHMENT.
DEININGER'S EXCELSIOR LUBRICATING AXLE.

CAUTION: Do not use grease for axles that require oil. They will seize-up eventually.

COACHES, CARRIAGES, AND CARTS: TYPE, USE, DESIGN, AND INDUSTRY

springs

THE TILBURY SPRING

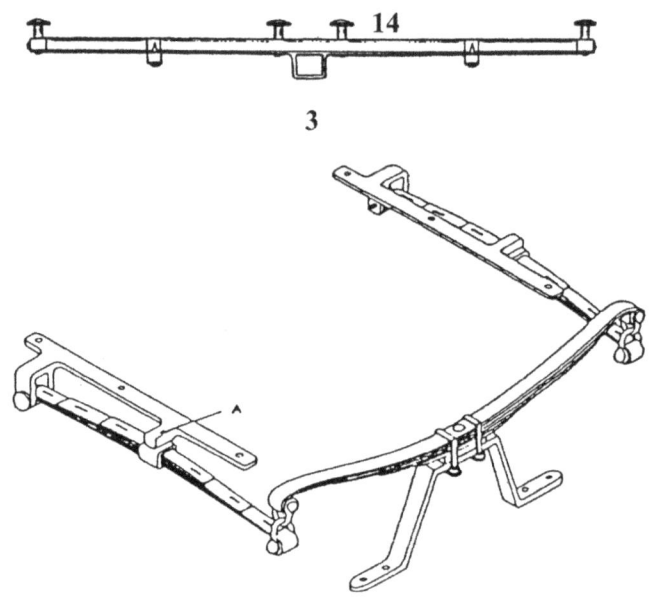

The **Tilbury Spring**, also known as the Gallows Spring, is a combination of three springs. An elliptic spring, with a double sweep, is hung on a metal bracket, ignominiously called a "gallows bracket." Two elbow springs are then attached to each eye, and to the body of the carriage. An Elbow Spring is really one half of a **Half-Elliptic Spring,** as specified in Obadiah Elliott's original patent.

HALF-ELLIPTIC SPRINGS

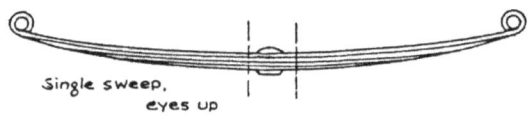

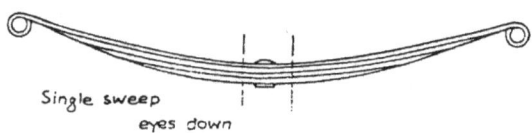

The **Half-Elliptic** is a leaf spring, which is the basic component of all other springs. The ends of the largest leaf are curled and the leaf spring is itself curled before the eye is rolled; it is said to have a Double Sweep and can help lessen excessive carriage movement.

THE ELLIPTIC SPRINGS

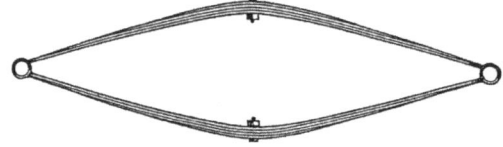

The combination of two half-elliptic springs produces the **Elliptic spring,** the most commonly used spring on most small carriages. One method used to date carriages is to examine the shape of the one master leaf and the manner in which it joins the opposing master leaf. To confuse matters, the half elliptic was also called the **Double Elbow Spring**.

THE TELEGRAPH SPRING

The **Telegraph Spring** is a combination of two half elliptic springs, sweeping up, and two half-elliptic springs, sweeping down. The four springs are attached together with a shackle. Since the springs created a sort of platform, it was also called a **Platform Spring** and, since it was commonly used on the Mail Coach, it was also called the **Mail Spring**. .

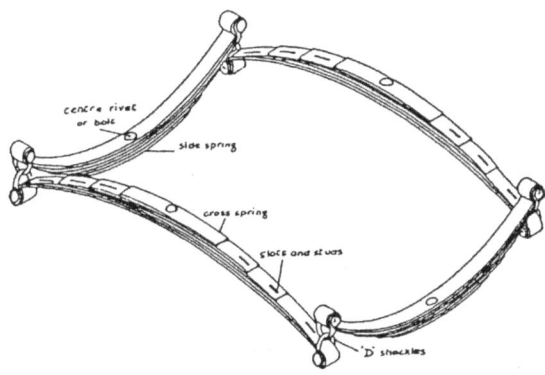

John Warde of Great Britain is credited with this suspension system. He found the coach box which rested on the front axle extremely uncomfortable and remedied this by placing a system of four sets of leaf springs between the front axle and the box seat. Warde persuaded the Manchester Telegraph to try his invention and they found the coachmen did not fall asleep and driving was easier. The name of the coach, Telegraph, became forever associated with this type of platform spring.

THE THREE-QUARTER ELLIPTIC AND CROSS SPRING

When heavier carriage bodies needed additional support, two elbow springs were added. This created the **French-Platform Spring,** and it was referred to as a five-spring suspension system.

THE THREE-SPRING PLATFORM OR DENNETT SPRING

When one of the elliptic springs were removed from the Platform Spring, and the ends of the half-elliptics were attached to the body of the carriage by a metal bracket, it was then called a **Three-Spring Platform Spring**. Since this spring was supposedly first used on a Dennet Gig, it is also known as the *Dennet Spring*.
All half-elliptic springs in the combination have double sweeps.

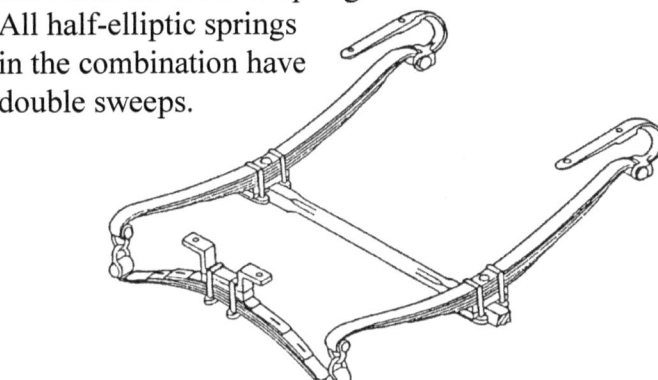

The C-Spring

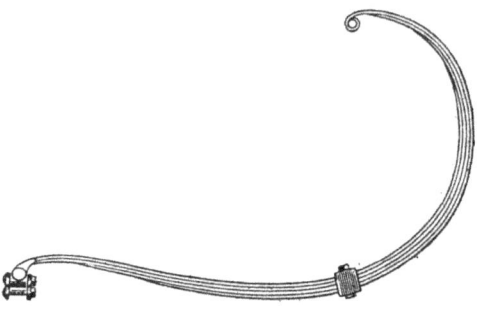

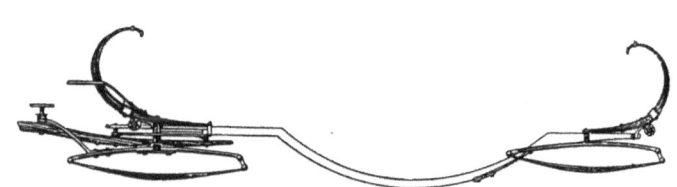

The C-spring developed from the S-spring, which had been commonly used to hang bodies on eighteenth century vehicles. The first modification was to turn the head down, creating the **Crane-Neck Spring**. From that, it was only a matter of time, before the spring was bent over into a C shape. Using such springs necessitated the use of sway straps to prevent the carriage body from swaying violently.

The most elegant spring combination, and the most comfortable was the **Eight Spring Suspension System.** Four C-springs were used together with four elliptic springs to create a superb spring suspension system. To prevent excessive spring movement, the leaf spring, which normally forms the top of the elliptic spring, was replaced by a dumb iron.

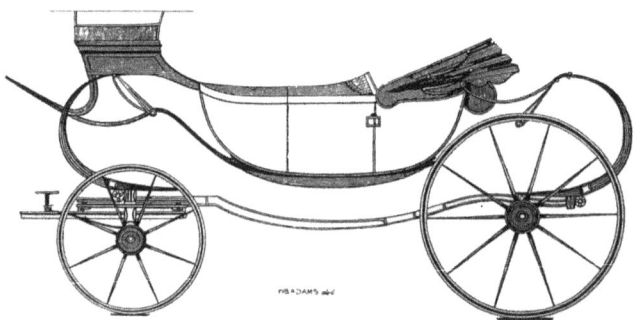

THE SWEDISH STATE COACH

This magnificent vehicle was built in 1897 for the Jubilee of Oscar II. It also has a double suspension, or **Eight Spring Suspension System**.

THE IRISH STATE COACH

This beautiful coach, which has a double suspension, or an Eight Spring Suspension System, was built by John Hutton & Sons (Dublin, Ireland) in 1851. It was destroyed by fire in 1911, at the coach factory of Barker & Co. This company rebuilt the coach from photographs, using the original irons. It is usually used for the State Opening of Parliament each year.

The Wheel

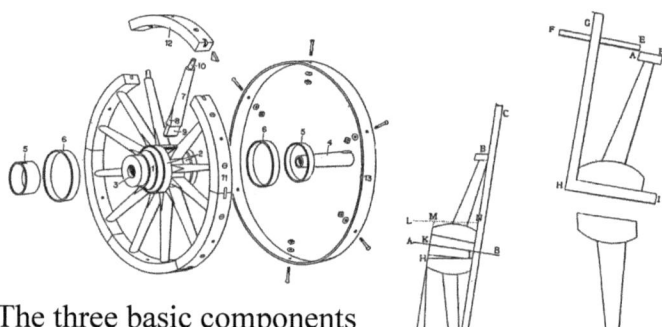

The three basic components are the *Hub, Spokes*, and the Felloes. The **Hub,** made of oak in England and elm in America, is the vortex around which the spokes are arranged. The **Felloes** form the rim of the wheel and are upon that rim that the wheel rides. It was later covered with iron tires to protect it from damage. At first, strips of iron, called strakes, were nailed on to this rim. An iron band, or hoop, was then put around the rim, and shrunk onto it to hold the whole wheel together.

The process of tiring a wheel is very precise work, although simple in execution. The iron hoop is heated to a certain temperature and when hot enough dropped over the wooden rim, hammered into place and cooled by throwing water on it. This causes the iron to shrink onto the wooden rim.

The **Spokes** of a wheel do not enter the hub or the felloe at a straight angle. They enter at a slight angle, sometimes no more than one-eighth of an inch. The measurement depends upon the diameter of the wheel. This causes a slight concave shape to the wheel, which is called a **Dish**. It prevents the spoke from breaking through the sidewall of the felloe when the wheel is raised up by a stone during travel, which it would do if the spokes entered at a ninety-degree angle.

THE FIFTH WHEEL

It is readily evident that a vehicle has either two or four wheels. However, a four-wheel vehicle actually has another "wheel" assembly, which permits the front axle to turn. The mechanism that achieves this is called the **Fifth-Wheel**. In some instances, when the unit has large metal rings, somewhat resembling a wheel, it allows the axle to turn. In other cases, it is composed merely of two small metal plates.

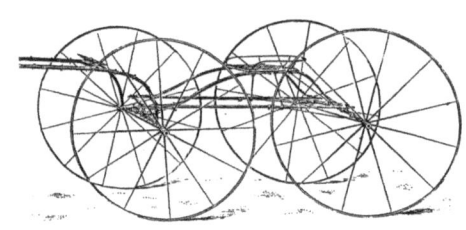

As industrialization marched forward, inventors did not forget the carriage industy. Machines for boring hubs, setting spokes, setting tires, bending tires, tenoning spokes and applying rubber tires to channels, which now circled the felloes were created by inventors to accomplish every task facing the carriage builder.

PATENT WHEELS

SARVEN WHEELS

James D. Sarven secured a patent for building a better wheel. He set the spokes into mortises in the hub, and then slid a metal flange onto the hub in front of the spokes, and another behind the spokes. Bolts were run through the spokes and the flanges tightened against them. The use of this metal support provided a very strong wheel, with very tight spokes.

There were many varieties of patented wheels following the Sarven patent. There was the Palmer Patent Wheel and the Archibald Wheel, both of which employed an iron flange to secure the spokes in place.

WARNER WHEELS

The Warner Wheel used a cast iron set of sockets, into which the spokes were driven. Since it was wood against metal the spokes tended to loosen, and could only be retightened once or twice before the wheel had to be replaced.

The simple band hub outlasted all the patent wheels. However, today the vast majority of buggy wheels are patent wheels of the Sarven type.

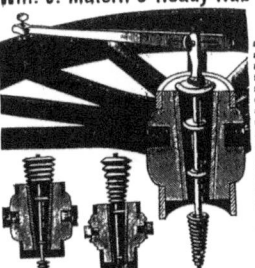

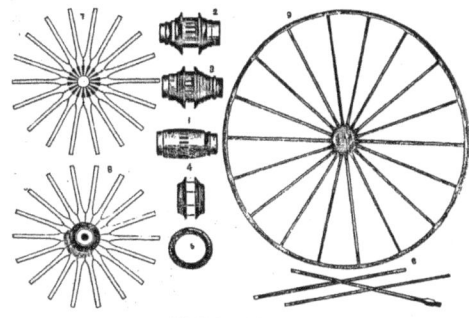

COACHES, CARRIAGES, AND CARTS: TYPE, USE, DESIGN, AND INDUSTRY

The Forecarriage

Beneath the carriage body is the undergear or undercarriage (or simply carriage), consisting of the running gear and chassis. The wheels and axles, in distinction from the body, are the running gear. The wheels revolve upon bearings or a spindle at the ends of a bar or beam called an axle or axletree. Most carriages have either one or two axles. On a four-wheeled vehicle, the forward part of the running gear, or **Forecarriage**, is arranged to permit the front axle to turn independently of the fixed rear axle. In some carriages a dropped axle, bent twice at a right angle near the ends, allows for a low body with large wheels. A guard called a **Dirtboard** keeps dirt from the axle arm.

In America, when speaking of heavy wagons and stage coaches, the inside futchells are called **Hounds**.

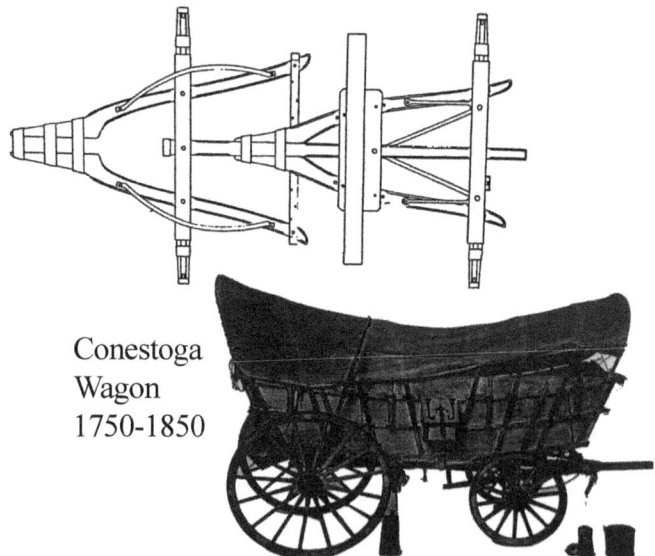

Conestoga Wagon 1750-1850

THE PANEL-BOOT VICTORIA

A. B. Footboard
1. 2. Bracket
3. Boot side
4. Seat valance
5. Heelboard
6. Seat rail
7. Long driving-box
8. Driving cushion
9. Lamp
10. Folding seat
11. Pillar
12. Quarter panel
13. Folding head
14. Seat squab or cushion
15. Seat fall
16. Quarter squab
17. Back squab
18. Dress preserver, wing, mud-guard or dasher
19. Step
20. Dress preserver or wing
21. Bottom-side
22. Footboard stay
23. Centre framing-piece
24. Wheel plate
25. Futchell
26. Futchell end
27. Wheel iron
28. Wheel-iron stay
29. Futchell stay
30. Top bed or transom
31. Bottom or axle-bed
32. Horn bar
33. Elliptic spring
34. Felloe
35. Tyre
36. Spoke
37. 38. Stock, nave or hub
39. Axle cap
40. Axle
41. Pump handle, body loop or hind spring stay
42. Hind spring bed or bar
43. Felloe piece or sweep piece
44. Head prop

**A Treatise on the Underworks of Carriages
by G. F. Budd - 1879**

18   COACHES, CARRIAGES, AND CARTS: TYPE, USE, DESIGN, AND INDUSTRY

There are two methods of attaching the splinter bar to the forecarriage.

METHOD 1

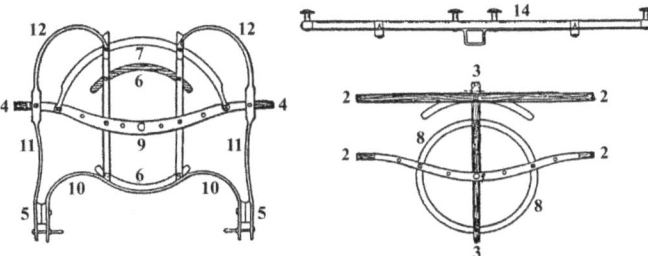

When the splinter bar can be removed, and a provision made for attaching thills, the futchells are said to be open. They are also called outside futchells. The carriage can be used either with a pair, or with a single horse.

1. Top bed, or transom
2. Horn - bar
3. Framing piece, or tongue piece
4. Bottom, or axle-bed
5. Futchells
6. Felloe pieces
7. Sway-bar, or sweep piece
8. Wheel plate
9. Perch-bolt
10. Front stay
11. Wheel iron
12. Hind stay
13. Shaft
14. Movable splinter-bar and pole are used for a pair of horse

METHOD 2

When there is no provision for removing the splinter bar, it is said to be fixed, and the futchells are said to be closed. The carriage has only a pole, and can only be used with a pair of horses.

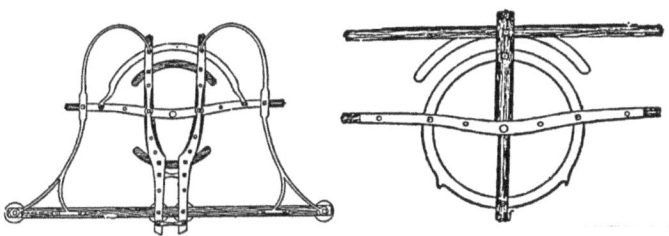

Ironmongers offered many different styles of forecarriages, each with subtle differences. They also came in different weights, to accommodate lighter or heavier carriages.

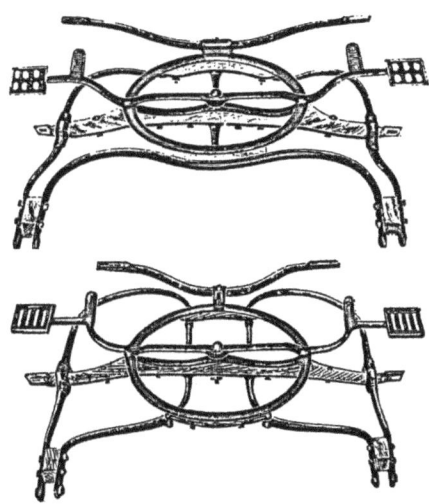

Two styles of Fore-Carriages for Stanhope Phaetons Four Wheel Dog Carts Light Wagonettes & C.

COACHES, CARRIAGES, AND CARTS: TYPE, USE, DESIGN, AND INDUSTRY

Two-Wheel Vehicles

The earliest vehicles had only two wheels. The body was placed upon an axle without any benefit of springing. Such design lasted all though vehicle history, as evidenced by this **Studebaker Dump Cart**.

As improvements were made in various types of spring design, they were quickly adapted to carriage designs by the various carriage makers. The **Village Cart** has three springs, two half-elliptic springs mounted perpendicular to the axle, the front of which are attached to the shafts. At the back is a half-elliptic spring with a double sweep.

The **Tandem Cart** is a form of the Dog Cart, only its body is set higher and is more substantial. It was adapted for **Tandem driving**, i.e. driving one horse in front of another.

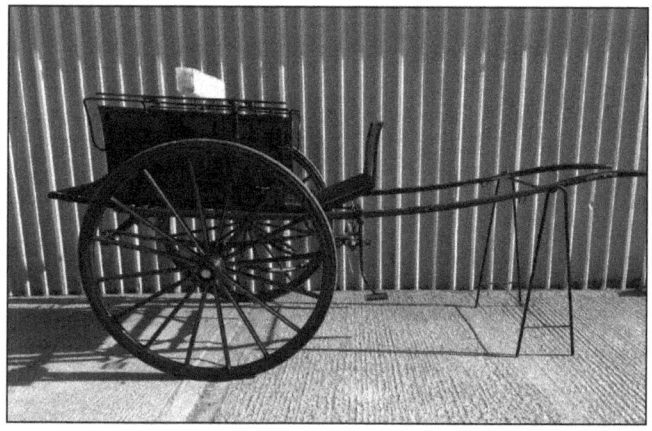

A **Four-Wheel Dog Cart** has four elliptic springs, one at each corner of the axle. This vehicle was very popular for use at country estates, and was adapted from the Dog Cart, a two-wheel vehicle.

A Stanhope Gig is the central feature of this print, The Derby Day-Tits & Trampers-On the Road to Epsom, painted by James Pollard, and published by R. Ackerman in 1842. The figure mopping his brow is said to be Pollard himself.

Below is the **Governess Cart** a vehicle hung on elliptic springs and a crank axle, which allows the body to hang lower.

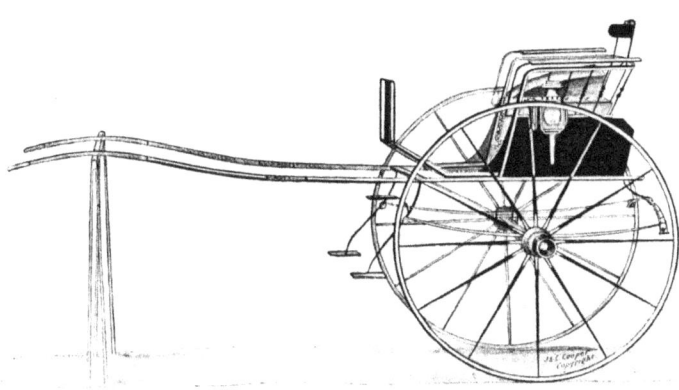

The **Stanhope Gig** is marked especially by the use of the **Platform Spring**, which is two half-elliptic springs perpendicular to the axle and two half-elliptic springs parallel to it. Such a form of springing was also called a Telegraph Spring or a Mail Spring since such springs as these were used on Mail Coaches. Another mark of the Stanhope Gig is the use of the Stanhope Pillar at the front of the body.

On the bottom right is a Rallie Car, distinguished by the rolled sides of the body.

COACHES, CARRIAGES, AND CARTS: TYPE, USE, DESIGN, AND INDUSTRY

Four Wheeled Dog Cart.

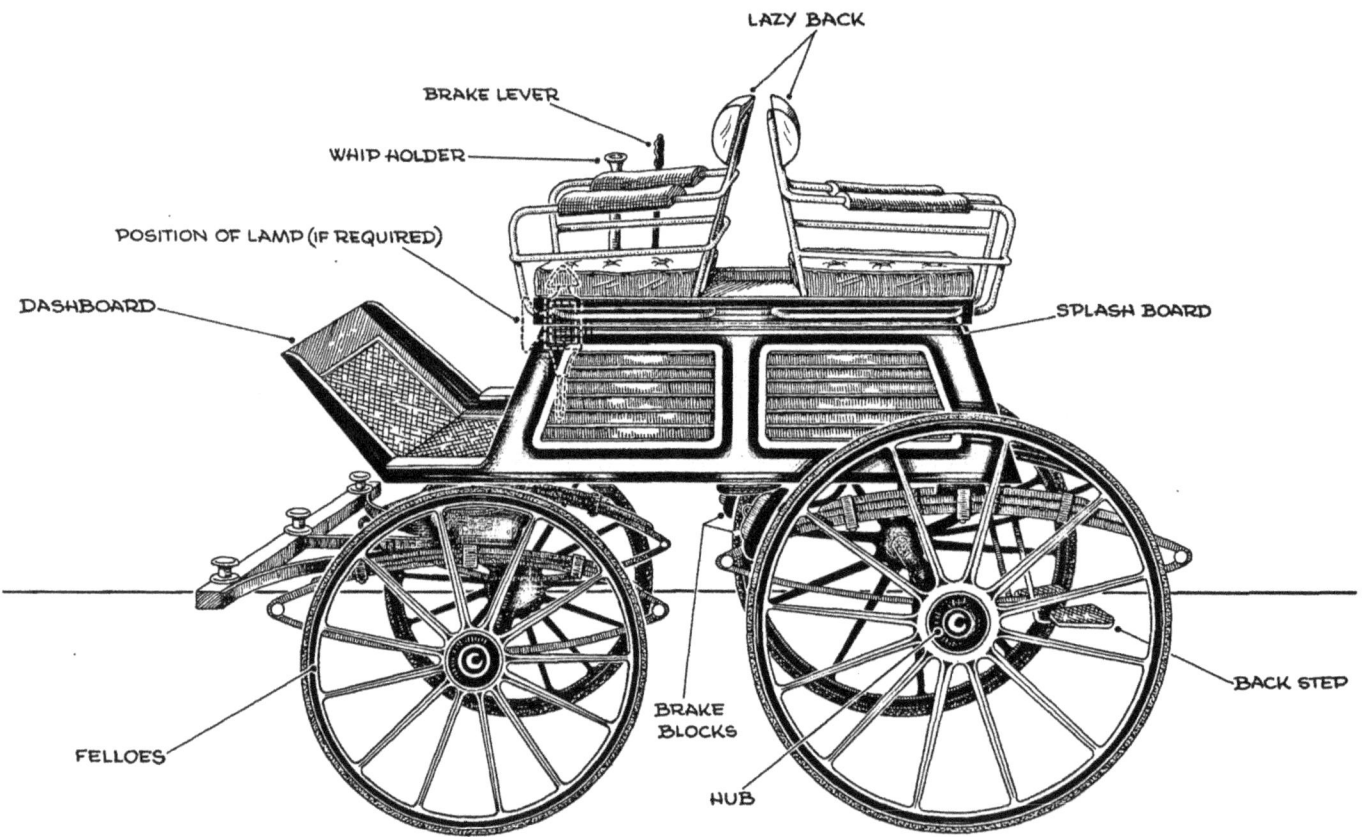

A Gig

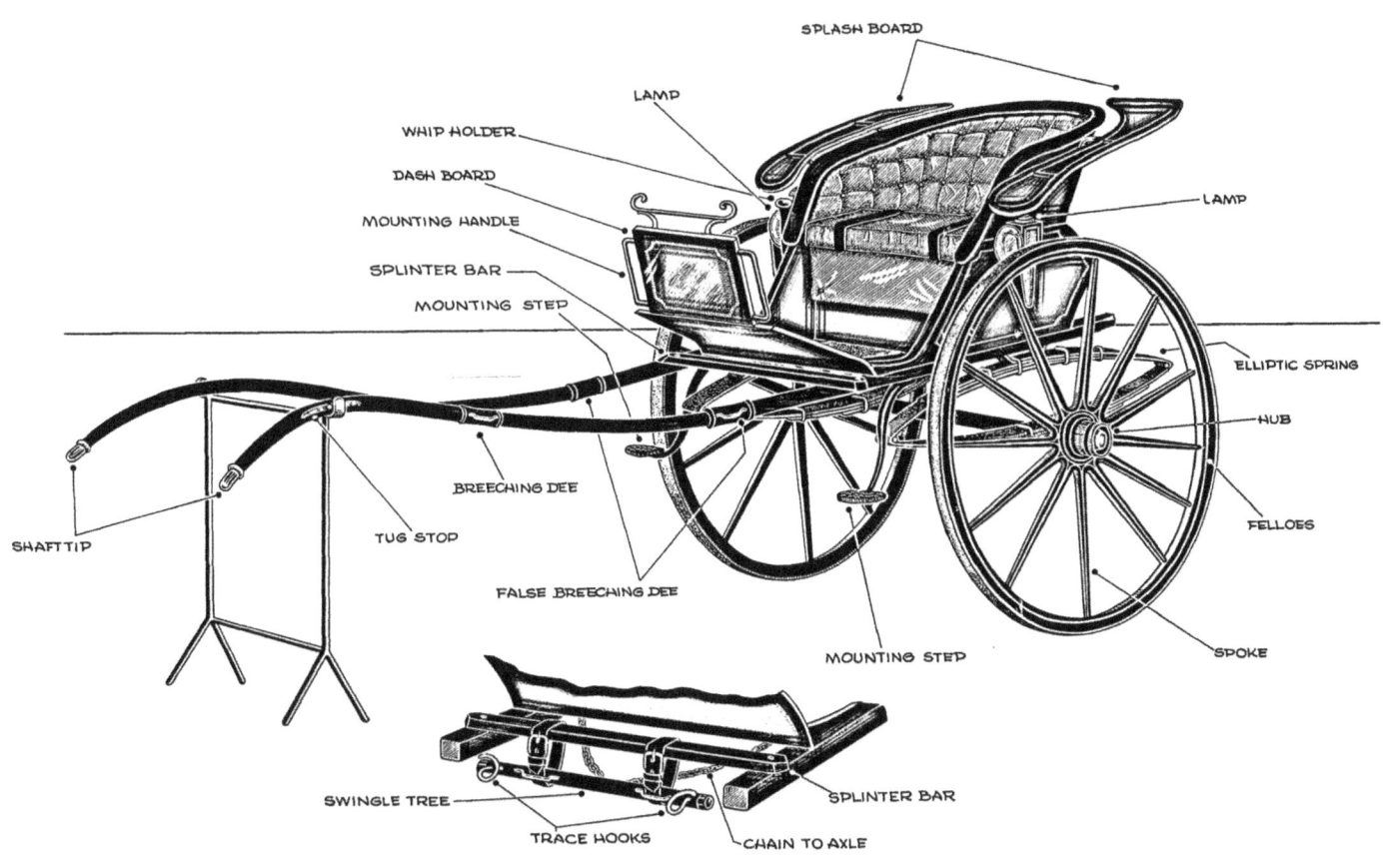

Carriage Tops

The most common form of carriage top is the Three-bows top. This was developed from the French closed top called a clash.
Goddard Buggy with Clash
It was commonly used on Runabouts and often called a Buggy.

The Standing Canopy Top, fittingly decorated with fringe, became the accepted top for a Surrey but was available as an option for other vehicles as well. Such a top was also fitted to a
Surrey or a Park Phaeton. It was extended from the back seat to the front seat, and the vehicle was therefore called an Extension-top Surrey.

The Parasol Top came down from the parasols placed on top of the Carrousel wagens in Europe, where it characterized a carriage intended for a lady to drive.

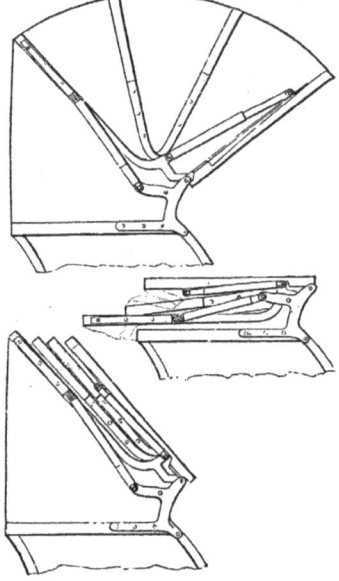

THE HEAD LIFT

There was great interest in having tops rise or lower without much effort. As a result, springs were loaded in tubes and placed beneath the leather top along with the bows. No prop showed outside the hood.

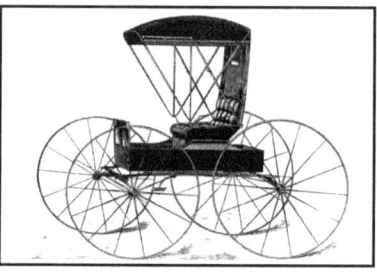

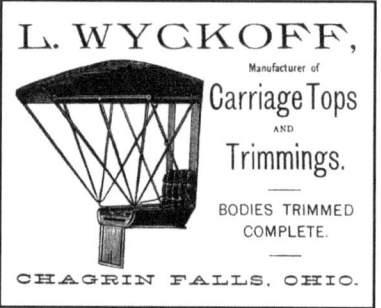

24 COACHES, CARRIAGES, AND CARTS: TYPE, USE, DESIGN, AND INDUSTRY

Six-Passenger Rockaway With A Hard Top

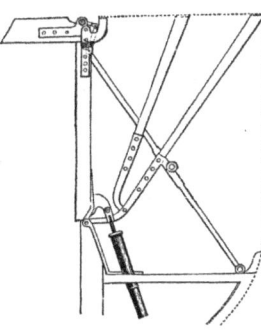

The "Climax" Head Lift

The Landau, with hood up

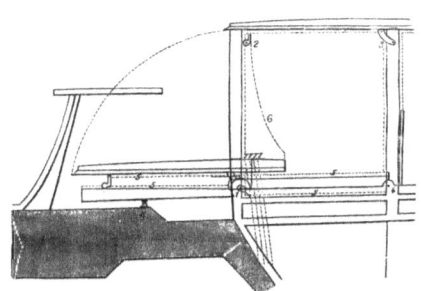

Mechanism For The Front Top Of Cunningham's Five-Glass Landau

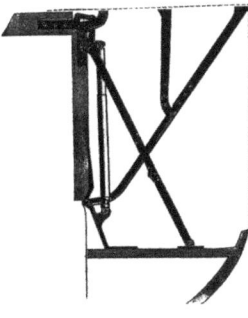

The "Euston" Head Lift

The Landau, with a folding hood

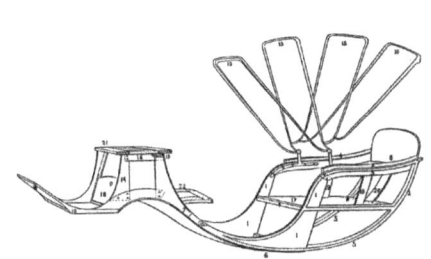

The Arrangement Of Bows For A Victoria Top

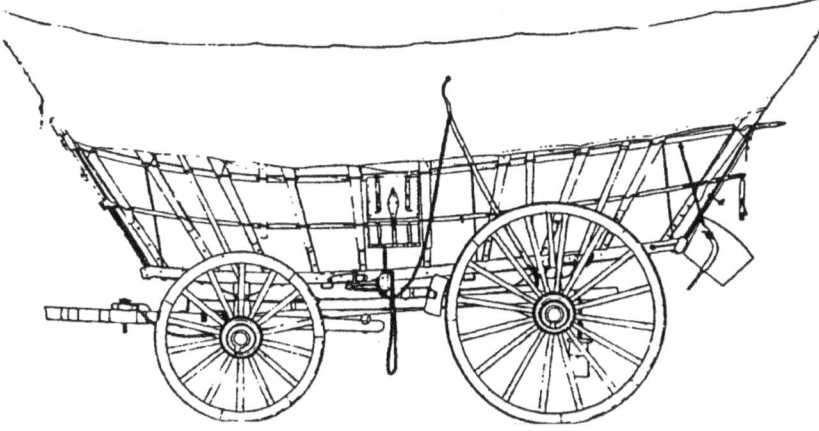

Conastoga Wagon with bows supporting the canvas top

COACHES, CARRIAGES, AND CARTS: TYPE, USE, DESIGN, AND INDUSTRY

Carriage Lamps

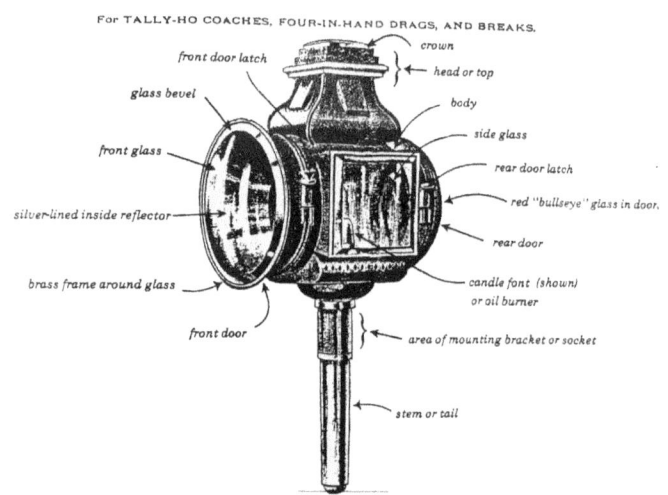

A CARRIAGE LAMP EXPLODED

Lamps were placed appropriately at different places on carriages. The design of the carriage often included the lamp bracket as part of the vehicle and required a lamp to complete the over-all design. Thus, one finds lamps mounted on dashboards, in front of dashboards, at the sides of seats, on the boots, on the front wall of the carriage body, or on the upper quarter of the coach body.

There were many styles of lamps. Like all of driving accouterments, there were some more formal than others. The Square Lamp was considered appropriate for a Victoria or Brougham; the Round Lamp was more sporting, and therefore was considered appropriate for a Break or Phaeton. Very ornate, plated or gilt lamps were put on State carriages.

There were many parts to a lamp, all soldered together into a complete unit This illustration shows the different parts of a single lamp.

One of the more beautiful accessories for a carriage was its lamps. Although they did not really provide light for any great distance, they served to warn others that a turn-out was ahead of them.

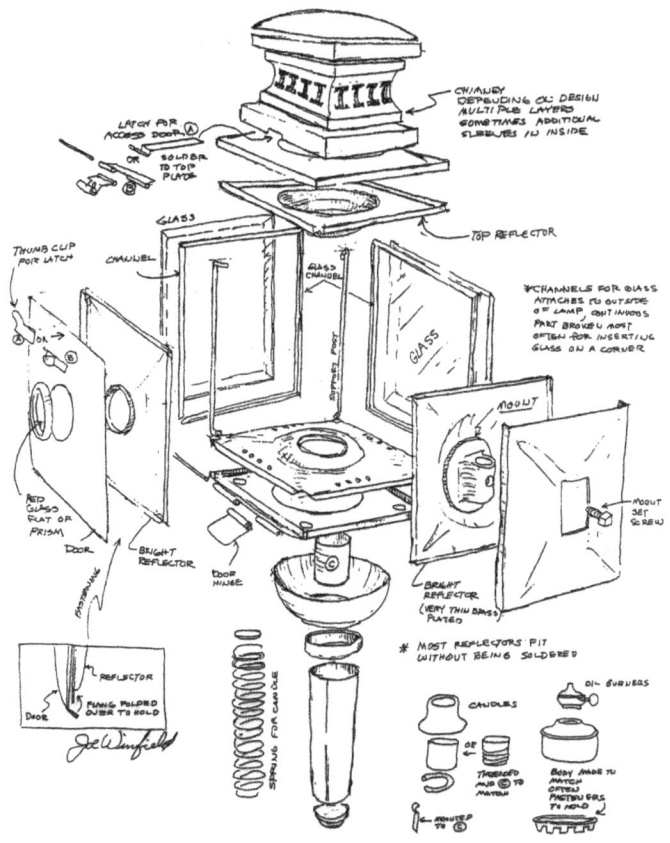

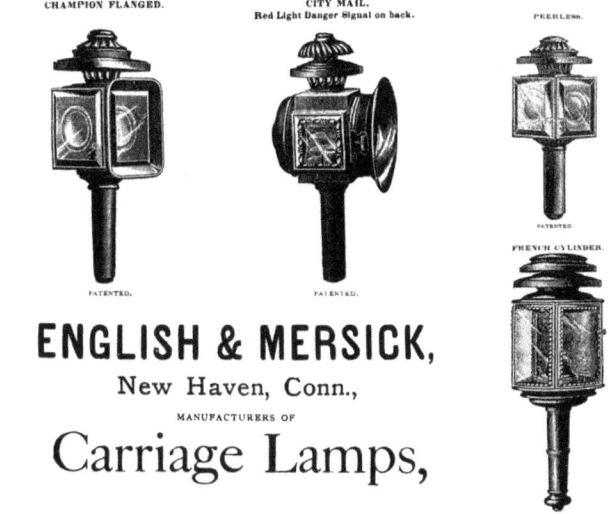

Major lamp-makers vied with each other in having the latest, up-to-date models in their catalogs. Cowles, or White & Co. or Devoursney Bros. were major lamp-makers. Carriage makers, such as Brewster Barker, and Studebaker, had lamps made with their company name on them.

COACHES, CARRIAGES, AND CARTS: TYPE, USE, DESIGN, AND INDUSTRY

The Breaks

Driving four-in-hands required the training of four-horse teams and exercising them well. Various types of carriages were designed for this work, and in turn became accepted forms of sporting vehicles themselves.

FOUR-IN-HAND HARNESS.

Four-in-hand harness was composed of four sides of harness. Two sides were for the wheelers, and two sides were for the leaders. As carriage driving became a popular pastime, and various rules were adopted for different turnouts, **Park Harness** was deemed more appropriate for a team pulling a Gentleman's Private Coach, or Drag. It was more elegant, and refined and showed more patent leather. Road Coach harness, on the other hand was somewhat more coarse, having been developed from the utilitarian harness of Mail Coach days. In due time, a certain elegance came to be expected even here. It is especially marked by the use of russet collars, and sometimes the addition of loin straps and trace carriers.

The Wagonette Break, with a second seat is also called a Built-up Break.

One of the pre-eminent forms of exercise vehicle was the **Wagonette Break**. The front seat accommodated the driver and passenger, and additional passengers sat behind facing each other on side seats. In time, a second seat was added behind the driver's seat. The Wagonette Break shown above has a perch; the one at the bottom right does not. The Wagonette Break was also properly called a **Body Break**.

Roof-Seat Break, a natural progression from the Wagonette Break, since no one really wanted to ride in the body any more. That was now only for the storage of horse blankets, driving rugs, headstalls and rain gear.

The **Break**, or **Skeleton Break**, the vehicle properly used for training teams of horses and to exercise them. There was a platform behind the driver's seat for helpers to ride and easily dismount. Sometimes, the weight of the vehicle was increased by adding a wooden box, filled with lead, to the back axle.

FOUR-IN-HAND COACH HARNESS.

The **Char-A-Banc** a heavy sporting Break distinguished by multiple seats. This was a heavy vehicle and could be used for long distance driving as well as exercising the four-in-hand.

COACHES, CARRIAGES, AND CARTS: TYPE, USE, DESIGN, AND INDUSTRY

THE PHAETON FAMILY

Many of the very fine carriages intended for their owner's personal driving were called Phaetons. The name was taken from the son of the Sun God, Helios, who drove his father's chariot of the sun across the heavens one day. The only common element among them all seems to be the fact they are owner-driven.

THE MAIL PHAETON

The largest of the Phaetons is the Mail Phaeton, which is an elongated Stanhope body set on Mail or Platform springs. The platform spring consists of two elliptic springs one way and two elliptic springs the other way, forming a square. The back spring can also be a Tilbury spring, a combination of springs set upon a "gallows bracket" invented by the coach builder, Tilbury.

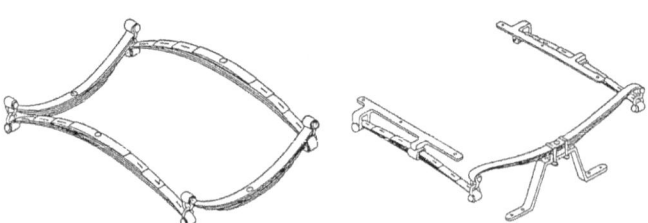

The Tilbury spring and arch, called a "gallows bracket".

THE DEMI-MAIL PHAETON

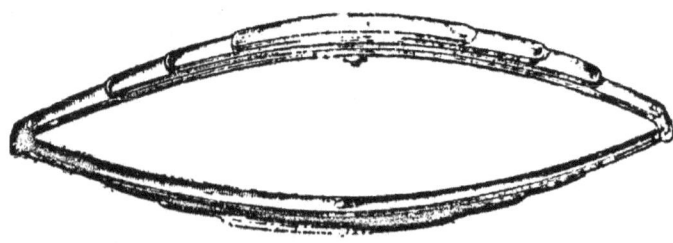

This vehicle has the same style body, but it is set on elliptic springs and does not have a perch

30 COACHES, CARRIAGES, AND CARTS: TYPE, USE, DESIGN, AND INDUSTRY

T-CART

THE STANHOPE PHAETON

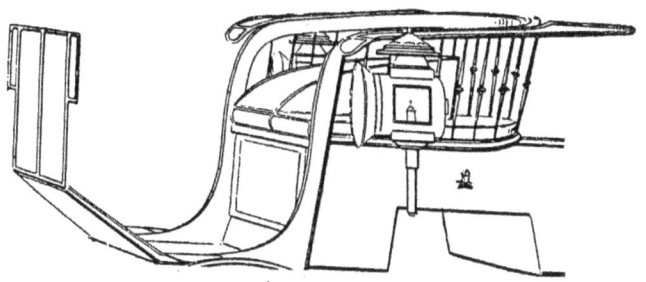

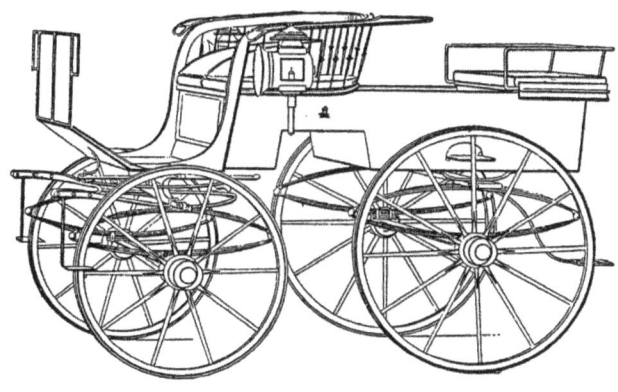

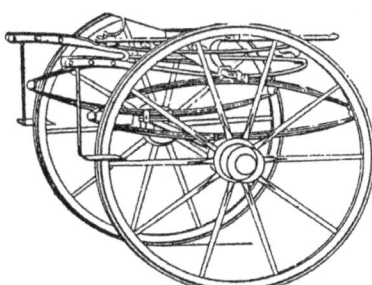

This vehicle has a body similar to that of the Stanhope Phaeton, but it has no top.

This vehicle has a cut-under beneath the front seat, and is also set on elliptic springs.

THREE WHEELED PHAETON

An article from Scientific American, 1856, featured this Improved Three Wheeled Phaeton. Invented by C.W. Saladee, editor of Coachmaker Magazine and practical carriage builder. He claimed the use of three wheels made it easier to turn the carriage and prevented contact between wheel and clothing when getting in and out of vehicle.

COACHES, CARRIAGES, AND CARTS: TYPE, USE, DESIGN, AND INDUSTRY

THE JENNY LIND

Fashion dictated that a lady should appear in public in proper dress, and suitable ensembles were made for her to go carriage driving. At first, she was only permitted to ride in the carriage, but later permitted to drive a carriage especially reserved for ladies.

P.T. Barnum

LADIES PARASOL WHIP

In keeping with her femininity, she carried appropriate accessories designed for females. Such was the Parasol Whip, invented in China, was required to keep the sun off as well as aid in driving. One sometimes wonders if it was at all practical.

Jenny Lind (1820-1887 was one of Europe's finest singers. She was brought to this country from her native Sweden by P. T. Barnum and she took the country by storm. Ships, songs, and carriages were named after her.

The Jenny Lind was a carriage characterized by a standing top, with two pillars at the back corners and two attached at the seat corners.

The parasol top was a particular characteristic of a carriage intended for a lady to drive.

LADIES WICKER BASKET PHAETON

LADIES DRIVING PARK PHAETON

COACHES, CARRIAGES, AND CARTS: TYPE, USE, DESIGN, AND INDUSTRY

THE CURRICLE

The vehicle known as a **Curricle** is actually a Chaise which has been adapted for driving a pair of horses to a two-wheel vehicle. The body is heavier and more substantial, and it is usually hung from C-springs on leather thoroughbraces. Many of them have a French hood, called a **Calash**. A dickey seat at the rear is provided for a groom, a diminutive servant who was called a **Tiger**. Only the coach houses of very prestigious and aristocratic persons contained a Curricle and they are very rare. It was replaced with the Cabriolet.

The vehicle had a **Pole**, positioned between the horses and suspended from a steel Curricle bar. It is mounted in terrets on the backpads of the horses' harness. This steel bar could slide to the right or left, since it was set on little rollers in the steel terrets. The backpads were larger and more substantial, six to eight inches in breadth. The Curricle was turned out with only the most spirited and imposing of horses, with great carriage and conformation, "perfectly matched in size, color, quality, and step." Until the dickey set was added, it was preceded or followed by two grooms mounted on another pair of horses equally well matched with those put to the carriage.

Curricle on display at the Shelburne Museum. built circa 1895 by J.B. Brewster & Company, New York

The **Terret,** with the steel rollers on which the curricle bar rode. It was mounted at the center of the packpad of the harness.

The Curricle Bar, shown mounted between the terrets.

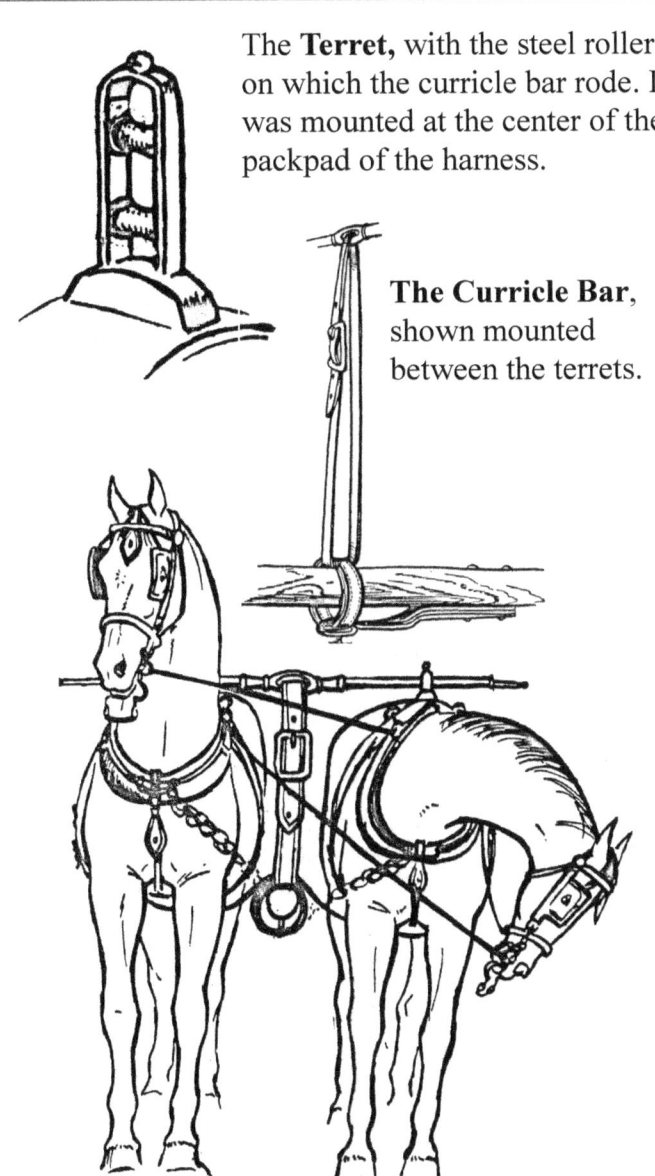

The Leather Strap which connects the pole to the center of the Curricle Bar. It is attached to a spring on the bottom side of the pole.

A Gentleman, his bays harnessed to a curricle. 1806, oil by John Cordrey c. 1765-1825

The curricle reached its height of popularity during the late 18th century and the early 19th century. Sometimes referred to as the "Age of Dandyism," ascribed to the British and commented on by the French. The curricle, well decorated, fit in well with the philosophy of the "Dandy." Charles Dickens, in his magazine, All The Year Round said this about the vehicle: "The curricle with ~ four horses and two servants to carry two persons in a carriage only fit for day-work was surely the height of extravagance."

The curricle as the fashionable carriage began to lose popularity around the 1830s. Perhaps because of the danger in two spirited horses pulling a medium weight, two-wheeled vehicle. Also, cabriolet at this time had much the same body as the curricle, making it a very stylish carriage, but it could be driven with only a single horse. As the curricle came to an end, a group of people maintained curricles throughout the rest of the 19th century, including the Duke of Wellington.

THE HANSOM CAB

The Cab is a corruption of the word **Cabriolet** a two-wheel carriage intended for the owner's private driving. Many second-hand Cabriolets were found eminently suitable for "taxi" work and the shortened word then came to identify them. The term was applied equally to two-wheel and four-wheel vehicles.

Hackney Cab, an old Chariot that has been pressed into livery work.

In 1834, Joseph Hansom received a patent for an improved cab. The unique feature of the vehicle was that the driver's seat was mounted above the passengers' seat and access to the passenger compartment was by two doors, which opened simultaneously. However, the wheels were huge being seven feet, six inches in diameter. In 1836 John Chapman improved the design by using a Crank Axle and lowering the wheels and placing the driver's seat behind the passenger compartment. F. Forder, a coach maker from Wolverhampton, England, perfected the design of the Hansom Cab even further.

Two popular vehicles are shown crossing Piccadilly Circus: a Cabriolet and a Stanhope Gig (From a print after G. Morton, engraved by Henry Aiken, and published by Thomas McLean in 1827).

To get about town quickly, catching a cab was the best bet. Cabbies plied their trade from cab-stands, not while moving. The fare was based on the distance. Passengers communicated with the driver and paid him through a trap-door in the roof. The cab-man controlled the door by means of a lever, which made it difficult to dodge paying the fare.

The Boulnois Cab was entered from the rear, but the cabbies found this rather inconvenient as fares quickly found it rather easy to skip by the back door without paying. This fanciful illustration is taken from Omnibuses And Cabs, H. C. Moore, 1902.

W.& F. Thorn exhibited a Brougham-Hansom at the Sportsman's Exhibition in London in 1887. It was an attempt to combine the elements of two popular carriages into one. Happily, the design was not well received.

COACHES, CARRIAGES, AND CARTS: TYPE, USE, DESIGN, AND INDUSTRY

PARK DRAG

Private coaches were first built for members of the driving clubs that were formed in London early in the 19th century, but only a small number were built before the time of the "coaching revival" in the 1860s. The chosen design at that time was based on a larger version of the Royal mail coach of 1835, and coaches made by the leading makers differed only in details. These coaches were used by two London coaching clubs for attending official driving meets. They were also used for driving to race meetings and other sporting occasions.

By BARKER & CO., LONDON

Exhibited by Million, Guiet & Co., of Paris, France

We consider this the finest of the four Four-in-hand Coaches exhibited. It is built after the English style, but presents considerable originality and great taste in its decoration and is distinguished, moreover, by the elegance of its proportions, and its lightness of construction, as compared with those of Messrs, Hooper & Co., and Peters & Sons. There are many fine points about it which show that the builders are thoroughly posted on this class of work.

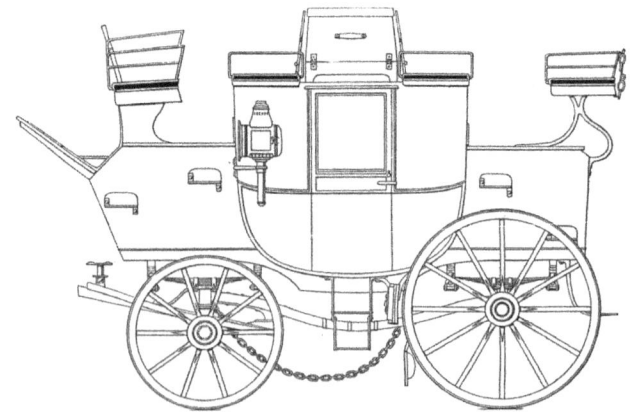

By BREWSTER & CO., NEW YORK

Rules for Judging Park Drags and Road Coaches as Adopted by THE COACHING CLUB

The Drag should have a perch and be less heavy than a Road Coach and more highly finished, with crest or monogram on the door panels or hind boot, or foot-board.

The axles may be either Mail or Collinges (not imitation).

The hind seat should be supported by curved iron braces, and be of a proper width for two grooms, without lazy-back.

The lazy-backs on the roof seats should be turned down when not in use.

The under side of the foot-board, together with the risers, should be of the same color as the under carriage.

The lazy-backs on the roof seats should be turned down when not in use.

The under side of the foot-board, together with the risers, should be of the same color as the under carriage.

The body of the Drag and the panel of the hind boot should correspond in color.

The door of the hind boot should be hinged at the bottom that it may be used as a table when open.

The skid and safety hook (if carried) should be hung on the off side. It is customary to trim the outside seats in either pigskin or cloth, and the inside of the Drag in Morocco or cloth.

The coachman's driving apron, when not in use, should be folded on the driving cushion, outside out. Passengers' aprons, if carried, to be folded and placed on the front inside seat.

There should be no luggage rails or straps on the roof between the seats.

Inside, the Drag should have: hat straps fastened to the roof, and pockets on the doors.
Places over the front or back seats where the lamps may be hung when not in use.

An extra jointed whip.

The umbrella basket, when carried, to be hung on the near side.

Lamps off.—Lamps inside coach.

Two extra lead bars, consisting of a main and side bar, fastened to the back of the hind seat with straps. Main bar above. Lead bars put on with screw-heads of furniture up.

The following articles to be neatly stowed inside the front boot:

A small kit of tools.

An extra lead and wheel trace.

A rein splicer or two double buckles of different sizes.

Extra hame straps.

Loin cloths for team and the necessary waterproof aprons should be carried in a convenient and accessible part of the Drag.

It is usual for a Park Drag to be fitted with luncheon boxes, wine racks, etc., also a box on the roof called an "Imperial." This latter is never carried except when going to the races or a luncheon.

COACHES, CARRIAGES, AND CARTS: TYPE, USE, DESIGN, AND INDUSTRY

ROAD COACH

Road coach is the term used in England for stage coaches running on a scheduled service and carrying fare-paying passengers. This name first came into use during the 1860s. Coaching enthusiasts, sometimes on their own account and sometimes as syndicates, put coaches on the roads running out of London in the summer months to some resort or beauty spot. Usually a coaching professional managed the operation and the amateur owner or syndicate provided the finance and covered any loss. Amateurs were in this way able to enjoy driving a coach in the old "down the road" tradition. Road coaches were built for this purpose and were similar in design to the park drags used by members of the coaching clubs, but of heavier build.

PUBLIC-COACH by BREWSTER & Co., NY.

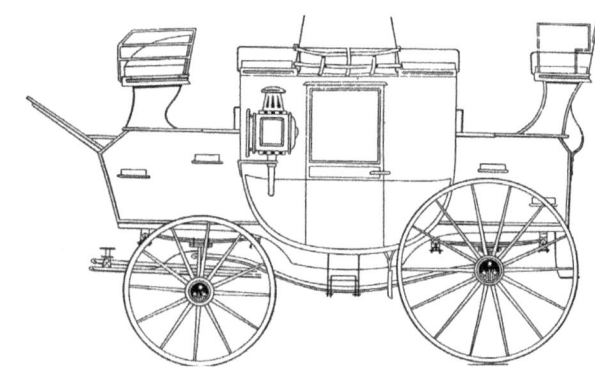

PUBLIC-COACH by F.R. SHANKS, LONDON.

PUBLIC-COACH by GUIET & Co., PARIS.

From Monday, April 10th, until Saturday, June 3d, 1899.

THE NEW YORK AND ARDSLEY COACH,

"PIONEER,"

WILL LEAVE

HOLLAND HOUSE,

DAILY, (Sundays excepted) at 10.00 A. M.

TIME TABLE AND FARES

MILES	FARES	LEAVING	TIME A. M.	FARES	RETURNING will leave	TIME P. M.
		Holland House	10.00		Ardsley Club	
6.2	$ .75	*Harlem	10.30		Ardsley	3.30
2.7	1.00	Washington Bridge	10.53	$ .25	Dobbs Ferry	3.40
3.6	1.50	*Kingsbridge	11.15	.50	*Hastings	3.50
1.	1.75	Van Cortlandt	11.20	.75	Glenwood	4.10
4.2	2.00	{*Yonkers } { Getty House }	11.40 / 11.45	1.00	{*Yonkers } { Getty House }	4.15 / 4.20
1.	2.25	Glenwood	11.50	1.25	Van Cortlandt	4.40
			P. M.	1.50	*Kingsbridge	4.45
3.8	2.50	*Hastings	12.10	2.00	Washington Bridge	5.07
1.6	2 75	Dobbs Ferry	12.20	2.25	*Harlem	5.25
1.7	3 00	Ardsley	12.30	3.00	Holland House	6.00
25.8		Ardsley Club				

Rules for Judging Park Drags and Road Coaches as Adopted by THE COACHING CLUB

The Road Coach should be built stronger than a Park Drag, especially as to the under-carriage and axles, which latter should not measure less than two inches in diameter.

The axles may be either Mail or Collinges (not imitation).

The hind seat is usually supported by solid wooden risers, with wooden curtain, but the supports may be of curved iron, as in a Park Drag, in which case a stationary leather curtain is used. Its seat should be wide enough for at least two beside the guard, who should occupy the near side with an extra cushion. He should have a strap to take hold of when standing to sound the horn.

The lazy-backs of the box-seat, hind seat, and roof seats are stationary. The under side of the foot-board, together with the risers of the box and rumble, should be of the same color as the under-carriage.

The body of the Coach and the panel of the hind boot should also correspond in color.

The door on the hind boot to be hinged on the off side to enable the guard to open it from the near hind step when the Coach is in motion.

The skid and safety hook must be hung on the off side in countries in which it is customary to drive on the off side of the roadway, for the skid should be on the outside wheel or the Coach will slide towards the ditch.

The iron rails on the roof, between the front and back seats, should have a lattice or network of leather straps to prevent small luggage, coats, rugs, etc., placed on the roof, from falling off.

Inside, the Coach should have: hat straps fastened to the roof, leather pockets at the sides or on the doors, and an extra jointed whip.

The basket shall be hung on the near side and in front of the guard's seat.

The horn should be placed in the basket with its mouthpiece up.

Side lamps in place and ready for use.

Two extra lead bars, consisting of a main and side bar, fastened to the back of the hind seat with straps. Main bar above.

Lead bars put on with screw-heads of furniture up.

The trimmings of the outside seats should be of carpet or any other suitable material, not leather.

The inside of the Coach is usually finished in hard wood or leather.

The coachman's driving apron, when not in use, should be folded on the driving cushion, outside out.

A foot-board watch with case should be provided.

The driving cushion should have a pocket on the side.

The following articles to be neatly stowed in a convenient part of the Coach:

A wheel jack. Extra hame straps. A chain trace. Extra lead trace. An extra bit. A bearing rein.

A rein splicer, or two double buckles of different sizes. A kit of tools, comprising a wrench hammer, cold chisel, coil of wire, punch, hoofpick and knife.

Two extra large rings for kidney links, or a pair of pole pieces.

The guard should be appropriately dressed and should have a way-bill pouch with a watch fitted on one side and a place provided for the key of the hind boot.

THE CHARIOT

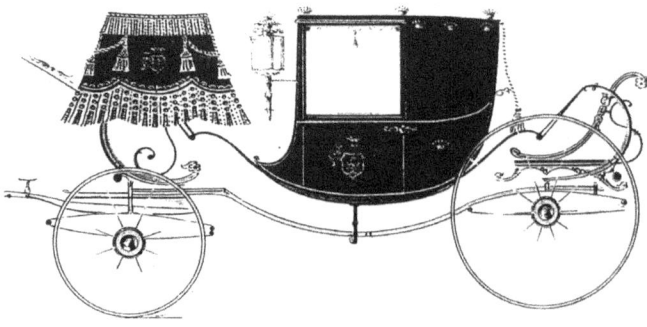

One of the very early types of carriages to be designed and to find favor with the aristocracy was the Chariot. It was a private, coachman-driven vehicle; its body hung on leather thoroughbraces from elegant C-springs. The panels were very finely painted and its owners' coat of arms was emblazoned on it in vivid colors. The coachman sat on an elaborately decorated seat, which was covered with a magnificent hammercloth.

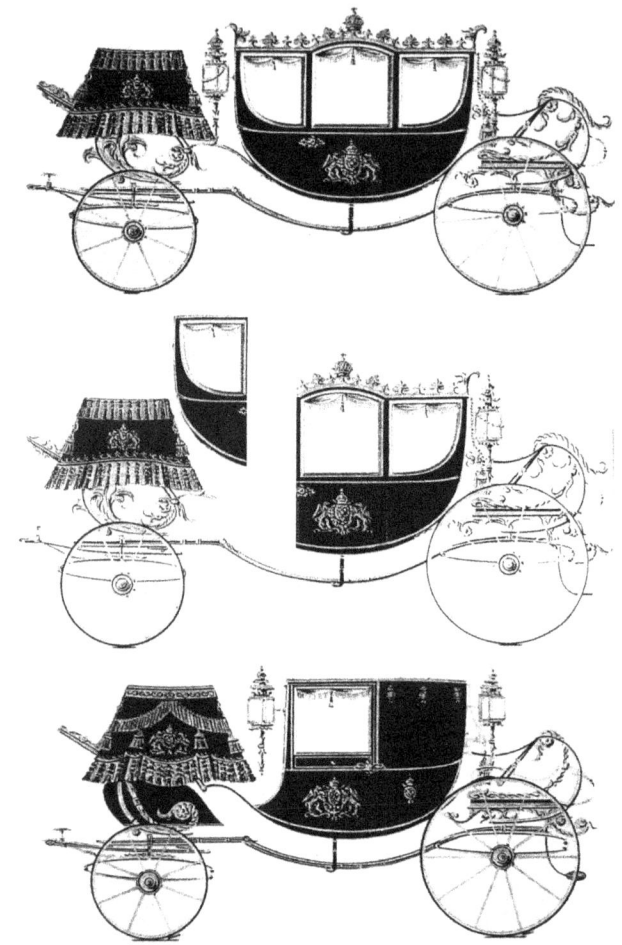

The Chariot accommodated two persons and was really developed from the Coach. By "removing" the front quarter section of the coach, a vehicle once accommodating four people was transformed into a vehicle now accommodating only two. Later, when this vehicle was supplanted by another carnage of similar, but less elaborate design, this concept was reinforced. It was called a Coupe i.e. a carriage cut from another.

42 COACHES, CARRIAGES, AND CARTS: TYPE, USE, DESIGN, AND INDUSTRY

The servants who accompanied such turn-outs wore elaborate **Livery**. Specific rules were set down for every occasion, and the each type of occasion required markedly different livery.

Carriages were not upholstered; they were trimmed. The craftsmen who did such work were called trimmers and they were highly skilled in the use of fabrics, laces and passamenterie. Books, such as Farr And Thrupp's Coach Trimming, were published to instruct apprentices and provide different patterns for seat cushions and backs. Pattern books provided several designs for customers to select from, and such designs ranged from simple and less formal patterns to very elaborate and highly festooned creations.

The coachmen from the Royal Mews in London wear the different royal liveries. They are, from the left, Scarlet, Full State, Plain and Semi-State.

Coats of arms were embroidered in gold or silver threads, or a coat of arms in brass could be attached to the fabric which covered a wooden frame. **Heraldry**, the complex and historic process of determining such coats of arms, provided all sorts of allegorical and fanciful designs, for such coats of arms.

COACHES, CARRIAGES, AND CARTS: TYPE, USE, DESIGN, AND INDUSTRY

THE DRESS CHARIOT

Specific types of horse-drawn vehicles began to emerge in the late sixteenth century. Among the very first was the **Chariot**, called a "charat" in Spenser's Faery Queen. In 1681, Mr. Maeares In St. Martin's Lane charged his client 23£.13s. 0d "for a little chariot." The Chariot belongs to that set of carriages, which are marked by "horizontal springs placed immediately on the axles, to intercept the concussion of the wheels, and sustain the whole weight of both body and carriage; a**nd circular upright springs, to sustain the body (Adams, English Pleasure Carriages)." This vehicle** became a mark of the aristocrat's coach house, and was always turned out formally, with liveried coachman and grooms. It came to be called a **Dress Chariot**.

The Dress Chariot in this collection was built by Armbruster of Vienna, circa 1850-60. It is thought that it was part of the "fleet" which served the Imperial court, and assigned to one or more of the Archdukes.

The Dress Chariot of the Emperor Franz Joseph I of Austria. Here it is shown turned out a la longsette, or Attelage a Huit a La Frangaise i.e. with a coachman driving six horses and a postilion driving a further lead pair. The vehicle is now in the Wagenburg at Schonbrunn, the summer palace of the Hapsburg Emperors outside Vienna. Franz

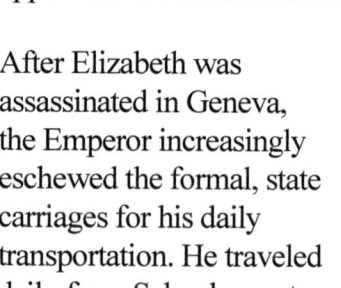

Joseph was a dedicated monarch, whose days varied little from day to day. Governed by very strict court etiquette, every move was surrounded by unvarying ritual. The State carriages and other vehicles which served the Imperial household were the direct concern of politically appointed Oberstallmeister.

After Elizabeth was assassinated in Geneva, the Emperor increasingly eschewed the formal, state carriages for his daily transportation. He traveled daily from Schonbrunn to the Hofburg and back again in this simply appointed Coupe (Brougham).

44 COACHES, CARRIAGES, AND CARTS: TYPE, USE, DESIGN, AND INDUSTRY

THE IMPERIAL WAGEN
Similar to the State Coach of Elizabeth II, a carriage known world wide, at the Royal Mews in London, the State Coach of the Hapsburgs was built in the middle of the eighteenth century and was used until 1916. It is a baroque carriage, heavily carved and gilt, with painted panels proclaiming the allegories of the empire.

SCHONBRUNN PALACE
Originally a hunting park, it was here that the emperor built a summer palace. Over the years it was greatly enlarged until it contained 1400 rooms. It was a favorite of all the Hapsburg rulers, who welcomed it as a grateful retreat from the Hofburg, the official residence of the Emperors in Vienna.

QUEEN ELIZABETH I
The Dress Chariot of the Empress Elizabeth. It was made by Cesare Sala, in Milan, and is also kept at the Wagenburg at Schonbrunn. It is slightly smaller than Franz Joseph's. The windows in the doors and upper quarter panel are slightly smaller, and there is a crest in the crest panel of the door.

This painting of the Imperial Wagen, drawn by eight white horses from the Imperial stud farm at Kladrub, accompanied by footmen in Spanish livery, was painted in 1763 by Franz Xavier Wagenschon.

COACHES, CARRIAGES, AND CARTS: TYPE, USE, DESIGN, AND INDUSTRY

THE COAT OF ARMS

In order to "read" the coat of arms, one has to understand the language of heraldry and know how to differentiate the various parts. The basic part of all coats of arms is the shield. The various symbols, colors and dividers are put on this. All the rest are appendages to the shield.

A coat of arms, so called because the heralds, whose responsibility it was to maintain the records of the granting of arms, wore them on their tabards (coats), is a complexity of various symbols, added periodically over a long period of time.

THE HONORS:
The most significant ceremonial objects connected with the coronation of a king comprise the "Honors."
In a grant of arms, supporters are sometimes given as a mark of distinction. The Shields of the Empire of Austria are supported by two Griffins, mythical Beasts, half lion, half eagle.

The basic shield in this coat of arms is an older, Renaissance-style, shield on which the double-headed eagle of the Holy Roman Empire is emblazoned. The Eagle holds in it talons The "Honors of Austria."

A second shield is conjoined on top of the first shield. On the second shield there are three further shields conjoined. Such conjoining is called marshaling of arms.

A sable (black) double-headed eagle, on a field of Or (gold), holds three of them: the scepter and the sword of state in its "left talons and the ORB in its "right talons.

The shield of the Dukes of Hapsburg: A Lion passant, Gules (red) on a field OR (gold). In the Austrian Coat of Arms, This lion is "Crowned."

The shield of the House of Lorraine, a bend Gules (red), on a field OR (gold), with three Silver alerions.

The shield of the Dukes of Austria, Gules (red) and Silver (white) in fess.

46 COACHES, CARRIAGES, AND CARTS: TYPE, USE, DESIGN, AND INDUSTRY

THE CROWN OF RUDOLF II
From 1804, the Crown of the Empire of Austria. Foremost among the "Honors" is the crown, which is not found on the shield, but surmounts the entire coat of arms.

THE IMPERIAL SWORD:
The sword was made of German steel, between 1198 and 1218. The sheath, dating from the 2nd third of the 11th century, was made in Germany, and was Byzantine enamel, plated with gold.

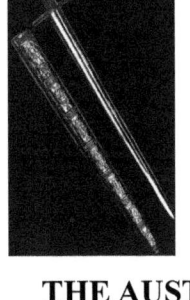

THE AUSTRIAN SCEPTER:
Made by Andreas Osenbruck, in Prague, 1615. The handle is made of narwhal horn.

THE AUSTRIAN ORB:
Believed to also have been made by Andreas Osenbruck, in Prague, between 1612 and 1615. Both the Scepter and Orb copy the style of the Crown.

The Emperor is the Grand Master of the Orders of the House of Austria. Foremost among these was the Order of the Golden Fleece. The Chain and Jewel of this order surrounds the conjoined shields of the coats of arms.

The jewels of the other orders hand from the base of the shield: The Order of St. Stephen, The Order of Leopold and the Order of the Iron Crown. The jewel of the Military Order of Maria Theresia, on its red and white ribbon, completes the ensemble.

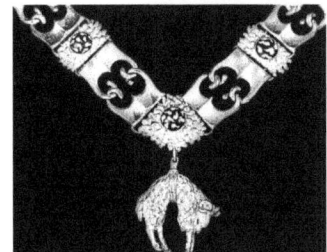

EMPEROR FRANZ I OF AUSTRIA
(1768-1835) wearing the Austrian imperial robes. The painting, done by Friedrich von Amerling in 1832, includes the "Honors of Austria."

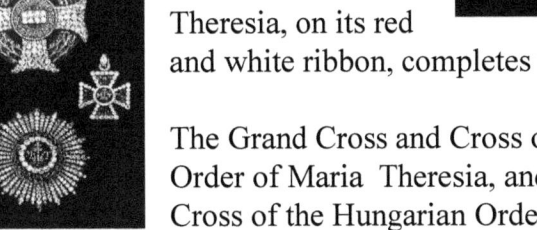

The Grand Cross and Cross of the Military Order of Maria Theresia, and the Star and Cross of the Hungarian Order of St. Stephen

THE ROYAL MAIL COACH

The development of multi-passenger vehicles began with the ungainly Diligence in France and the huge Mail Coaches of Switzerland and Germany. These were very large coaches with several passenger compartments, both inside and outside the coach.

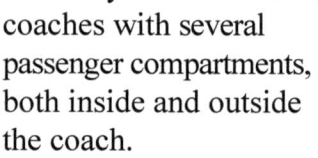

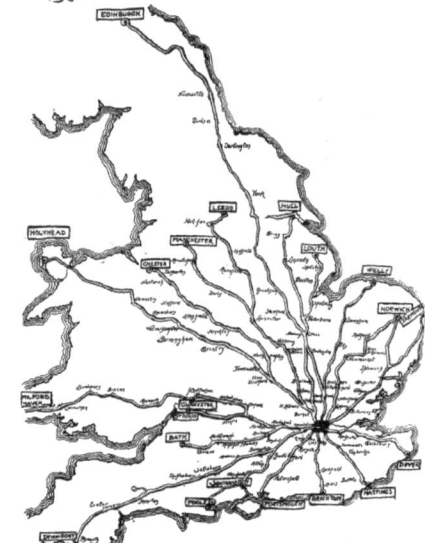

The Coachman.

In 1784, John Palmer, a theatre owner from Bath England, frustrated with the unreliable mail delivery system, designed a coaching system and developed a Mail Coach to make it work. The coach was patterned after the developing English Stage Coach. However, his introduction of a standard design with interchangeable parts contributed to making the Royal Mail Coach a success. By 1837, when the mail contracts were given to the railroads, the mail coach system, spread in every direction across England, was comprised of 180 different mail routes, using 150,000 horses and employing 30,000 men.

The British Post Office bought into the plan and the whole country was caught up in the movement of Mail Coaches all over England. The romantic era that followed was captured on canvas by C. Cooper Henderson, James Pollard and James Herring as well as others, and their paintings were made into "coaching prints," which are now highly prized by collectors.

The Guard, who was responsible for the mail was the sole government employee. The coach, harness, horses and coachman were all owned or hired by one or more, private entrepreneurs.

THE GUARD.

Depart from	Coach	Hour	Route	Arrive at	Time on Road	Return to London
Bell and Crown, Holborn	Alert	8.30 a.m.	...	...	7½ hours	8.30 a.m.
"	"	10.30 a.m.	...	...	7½ hours	4.0 p.m.
Old Bell, Holborn	"	8.30 a.m.	...	52 East Street	...	9.0 a.m.
"	Meteor (safety)	10.30 a.m. (not on Sunday)	...	...	...	...
Blossoms Inn	Night-coach	10.0 p.m.	...	...	8 hours	...
"	Blue coach	9.0 a.m.	Clapham, Sutton	...	7 hours	10.0 a.m.
"	True Blue	9.0 a.m.	Croydon, Ryegate, Crawley, Hickstead	...	6 hours	11.0 a.m.
"	Royal York	1.0 p.m.	...	...	6 hours	1.0 p.m.
Boar and Castle, 6 Oxford Street	True Blue	8.30 a.m.	...	...	...	...
"	Royal Eagle	12.30 p.m.	Horsham, Henfield, Shoreham	...	...	...
Bull Inn, Bishopgate	Royal Clarence	8.30 a.m.	...	...	...	...
Bull, Holborn	A coach	8.0 a.m.	Sutton, Ryegate, Cuckfield	Old Ship	7½ hours	9.30 a.m.
Bull Inn, Leadenhall St., and Old Black Boar	Royal George	7.30 a.m.	...	...	...	...
"	Royal Sussex	2.0 p.m.	...	...	6 hours	...
"	New Dart	10.0 a.m.	...	...	...	...
Cross Keys, Wood Street	Life Preserver	8.45 a.m.	...	...	...	...
"	Royal Clarence	8.30 a.m.	Horsham, Henfield	...	...	...
"	Times	2.0 p.m.	...	...	...	...
Flower Pot, Bishopgate	"	7.0 a.m.	...	...	...	...
"	Regent	8.0 a.m.	...	...	...	...
"	A coach	8.45 a.m.	...	...	...	...
Four Swans	"	9.0 a.m.	...	...	...	...
"	"	2.0 p.m. (on Sunday only, 9.0 a.m.)	...	...	...	...
George and Blue Boar	Post-coach	8.0 a.m.	Ryegate, Crawley, Cuckfield	Blue Office	...	...
"	"	9.0 a.m.	...	...	...	9 a.m. (8 hours)
Golden Cross, Charing Cross	Original Red coach	9.0 a.m.	Croydon, Ryegate, Crawley, Hickstead	The Castle	9 hours	6 a.m. (6 hours)
"	Eclipse	2.0 p.m.	...	"	7 hours	...
Shepherd's Office, 90 Bishopgate Street Within	A coach	8.30 a.m.	Croydon, Ryegate, Cuckfield	...	...	...
"	"	9.0 a.m.	Croydon, Godstone, E. Grinstead, Lewes	...	...	...
"	A light coach	9.30 a.m.	...	...	...	...
"	"	12.0 noon	...	...	...	...
"	"	2.30 p.m.	...	...	...	...
Ship, Charing Cross	A coach	9.0 a.m.	...	...	...	...
"	"	11.0 a.m.	...	...	...	...
"	"	1.45 p.m.	...	...	...	5.0 p.m. (6 hours)
Spread Eagle, Gracechurch Street	Sovereign	6.45 a.m.	Ryegate, Crawley, Hickstead	4 Castle Square	6½ hours	...
"	Defiance	...	...	...	6 hours	11.0 a.m.
"	Dart	2.45 p.m.	Ryegate, Crawley, Hickstead	...	6 hours	...
"	Comet	9.45 a.m.	...	...	7½ hours	10.0 a.m. (7 hours)
Swan with Two Necks, Lad Lane	Royal Brunswick	2.30 p.m.	...	135 North Street	6½ hours	8.0 a.m. (6 hours)
White Bear, Piccadilly	Rocket (New Road)	10.0 a.m.	...	...	6 hours	...
White Horse, Fetter Lane	Princess Charlotte	9.30 a.m.	Croydon, Ryegate, Crawley, Cuckfield	Old Ship	7½ hours	1.0 p.m. (7 hours)

COACHES, CARRIAGES, AND CARTS: TYPE, USE, DESIGN, AND INDUSTRY

EVOLUTION OF THE AMERICAN COACH BODY

In a seemingly short period of time, America transformed from a wilderness into a booming and bustling new country. Roads connected towns and stagecoaches traveled between the towns. As the country grew people headed west to start a new life. There were several routes to get to the west and, once there, people needed to travel from town to town and state to state just like they did in England. Railroads did not destroy the stage line business like it did in Europe though. Vehicles of all types and sizes were needed around the railroad heads to transport goods and people through the vast lands of the west. There were over forty different types of vehicles in use and over three thousand Concord coaches were made.

During the Gilded Age, late 1860s to 1896, America changed radically. After the westward expansion of the railroad and telegraph, the display of wealth manifested itself in the use of European inspired Park Drag and Private Road Coaches gracing the streets of America's big cities.

Coach Manufacturers

Jason Clapp - Pittsfield, MA
Charles Veazie - Troy, NY
Orsamus Eaton Uri Gilbert - Troy, NY
James Goold - Albany, NY
Abbot and Downing - Concord, NH

1760

The coachee was generally a private vehicle used in the colonies of the United States. With no glass, passengers were protected in bad weather by side curtains that are seen here rolled up to the roof. The cee springs front and back with leather thoroughbraces protected the body of the coach and the passengers from the jar of the road surface.

1795

American coachee, about 1795

50 COACHES, CARRIAGES, AND CARTS: TYPE, USE, DESIGN, AND INDUSTRY

1798

From 1798 until the end of his life, George Washington maintained a succession of fashionable carriages. None of them exist today.

1820

"The American Mail Stage in which we journeyed over so many wild as well as civilized regions, deserves a place at our hands. And if the sight of this Sketch does not recall to persons who have traveled in America the idea of aching bones, they must be more or less than mortal! The springs, it will be observed, are of hide, like those of the French Diligence—and every thing about it is made of the strongest materials. There is only one door, by which the nine passengers enter the vehicle, three for each seat, the center sufferers placing themselves on a movable bench with a broad leather band to support their backs. Instead of panels, these Stages are fitted with leather curtains. The baggage is piled behind, or is thrust into the boot in front. They carry no outside passengers—and indeed it would try the nerves as well as the dexterity of the most expert harlequin that ever preserved his balance, not to be speedily pitched to the ground from the top of an American coach, " From "Forty Etchings, from sketches made with the camera lucida in North America in 1827 and 1828," by Captain Basil Hall, R.N.

1827

The Concord coach was the most complex design of all stagecoaches. Concord stages were first to offer shock-absorbing thorough braces—an important feature not just for passengers, but for the animals pulling them, too. (cited from: https:// www.parks.ca.gov/?page_id=25449)

Gloria Austin's reproduction of the Concord Coach

1829

The American public "**Sociable**" was for public use and had windows and a rack for luggage and parcels on its roof. As roads improved, so did suspension systems on the coaches and carriages. The Sociable was suspended on cee springs.

COACHES, CARRIAGES, AND CARTS: TYPE, USE, DESIGN, AND INDUSTRY

THE CONCORD COACH

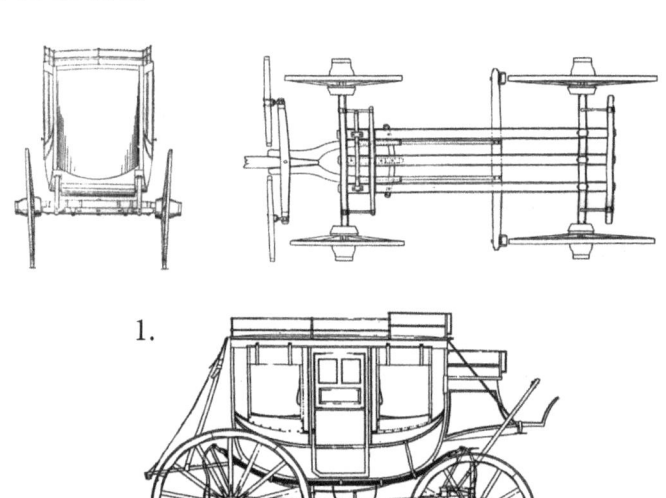

1.

2.

3.

In 1813, Lewis Downing moved to Concord, NH to build Pleasure Wagons and Sleighs. In 1827, he hired J. Stephens Abbot to help him build a stagecoach and they built three of them in the winter of 1827-1828. This new vehicle was gradually acknowledged as the archetype of the American stagecoach, known as the **Concord Coach**. It was offered in three sizes, a 6 Passenger, 9 Passenger and 12 Passenger, each denoting the inside passenger capacity. Typically, they carried additional passengers on roof seats and on the roof itself.

The Concord Coach was also offered in three styles: The City-style (1. top right) and the Western-style (2. right center). When French windows replaced the leather curtains, it was called a Hotel Coach (3.). The reaches of a Western-style coach are hung beneath the axle. A distinguishing feature of all Concord Coaches are the three reaches in the gear as depicted at the (top right).

DAILY OVERLAND MAIL
☛ THROUGH IN TWENTY DAYS! ☚

The Concord Coach became the preferred vehicle for western transport. Stage line owners proudly boasted in their advertising that their line used Concord Coaches.

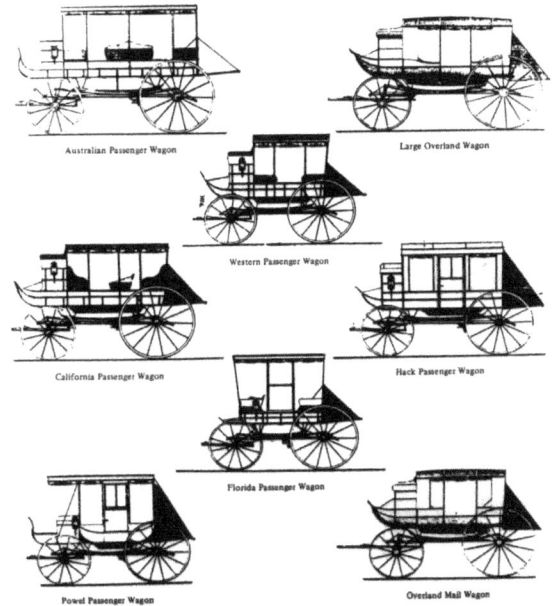

ABBOT, DOWNING & CO.
CONCORD, N.H.

- Australian Passenger Wagon
- Large Overland Wagon
- Western Passenger Wagon
- California Passenger Wagon
- Hack Passenger Wagon
- Florida Passenger Wagon
- Powel Passenger Wagon
- Overland Mail Wagon

The companies established by Lewis Downing and J. Stephens Abbot offered several, different models of coaches, in addition to their famous Concord Coach. Some of these are shown in the company Broadside shown above.

Shown above is the famous order for thirty Concord Coaches for the Wells Fargo Company, which was now running coaches on the Overland Mail route. The order lists the specific details for the building of coaches, including instructions to paint the body "RED" and the carriage "STRAW," and trim the coach in russet leather.

COACHES, CARRIAGES, AND CARTS: TYPE, USE, DESIGN, AND INDUSTRY

THE CONCORD COACH

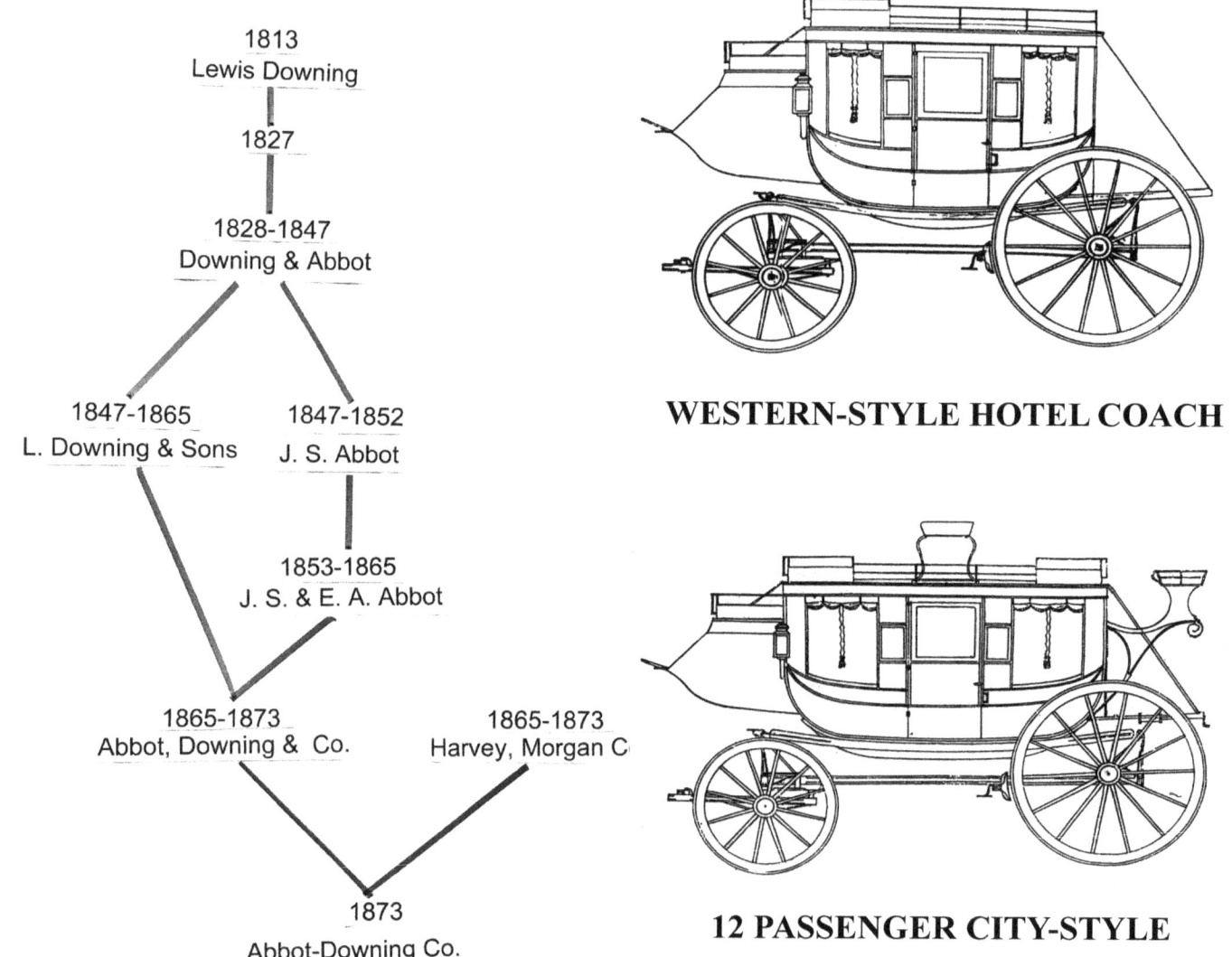

WESTERN-STYLE HOTEL COACH

12 PASSENGER CITY-STYLE

1813 Lewis Downing
1827
1828-1847 Downing & Abbot
1847-1865 L. Downing & Sons
1847-1852 J. S. Abbot
1853-1865 J. S. & E. A. Abbot
1865-1873 Abbot, Downing & Co.
1865-1873 Harvey, Morgan C[o.]
1873 Abbot-Downing Co.

HOTEL COACH

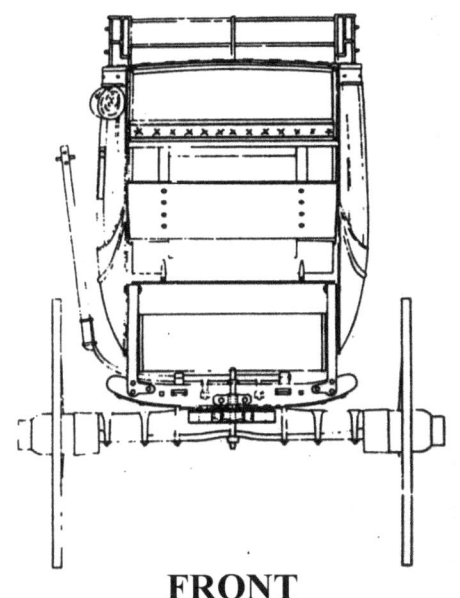

FRONT

CITY-STYLE

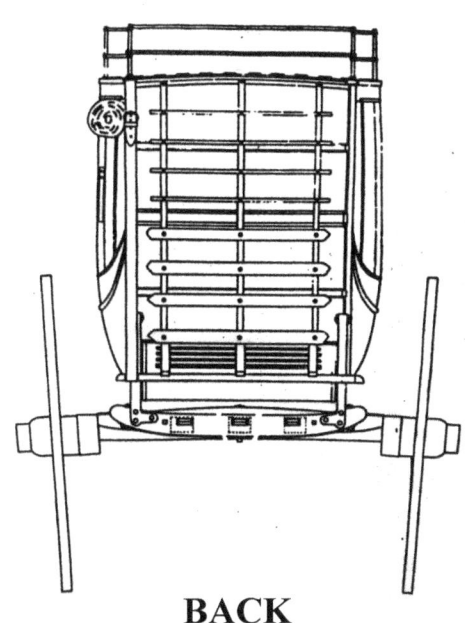

BACK

COACHES, CARRIAGES, AND CARTS: TYPE, USE, DESIGN, AND INDUSTRY

THE AMERICAN SLEIGH

Chores and the need to ready the fields, sow seed and take in the harvest kept Americans busy three seasons of the year. When winter came, they were ready to take advantage of the snow, to travel about and visit, and race and frolic. The sleigh was America's own.

ALBANY CUTTER
James A. Goold, a carriage manufacturer from Albany, New York designed a light, swell-bodied sleigh,  with a wooden dash, which curled up ad over the passengers knees. It accommodated two people, and quickly became one of the two most popular sleigh designs in America.

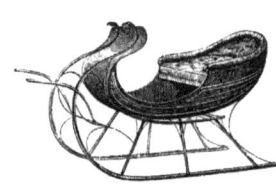
No. 184.—Albany Cutter.

PORTLAND CUTTER
Kimball Bros, from Portland, ME, Developed a square-bodied sleigh, which likewise came to dominate the sleigh market. For some reason it was never painted up as fancifully as the Albany Cutter, but it often did have quarter panels of contrasting colors.

No. 185.—Light Two Seat Sleigh.

Other carriage makers were quick to capitalize on Goold's successful design. Lawrence, Bradley & Pardee offered three models in its 1862 Catalog: a two-seat Cutter, a four-passenger sleigh, which had a jump seat, and a four passenger Pony Sleigh.

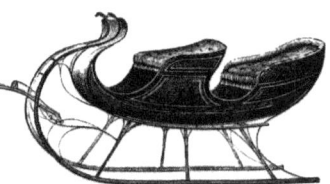
No. 186.—Fine Pony Sleigh.

QUEEN'S BODY CUTTER
Somewhat similar to the Portland, it does not have its harsh angular lines. The body is fuller and more commodious. It is well trimmed and exhibits the curved dash. The treatment of the knee irons is decidedly different in this particular model.

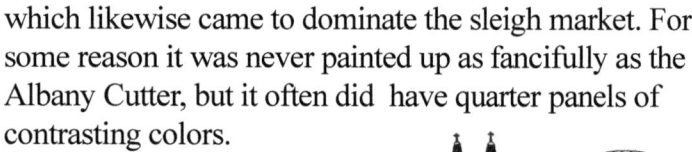

FANCY CUTTER
Marketed by Brewster of Broome St., New York, this sleigh was widely popular with the city crowd and could be found in Central Park, decked out in furs, horse-hair plumes and bells, and driven by the many sleigh fanciers among New York's elite.

56 COACHES, CARRIAGES, AND CARTS: TYPE, USE, DESIGN, AND INDUSTRY

The first sleighs in America were the pung and its near relatives, pods, podangers, and travis sleighs. The Country Sleigh, 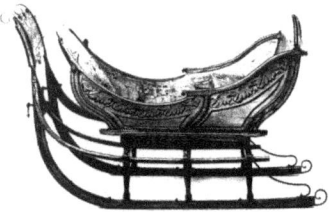 which dominated the sleighing scene for the first half of the nineteenth century had a bath-tub shaped body, fastened to the conventional three-knee frame common to work sleds and pungs.

The Albany Cutter was decorated in all manner of fancy designs, with painted quarter panels on its sides, and the back was usually embellished by a lovely landscape scene.

BOSTON BOOBY
Called simply a Booby Hut, this sleigh was the creation of Chauncey Thomas, a carriage maker from Boston. As the 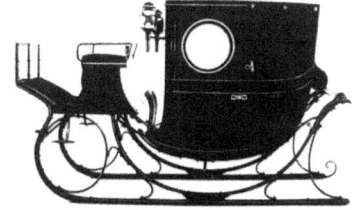 Chariot became obsolete, families, which owned one, were left with it standing uselessly in their coach houses. Thomas created a hoop-shaped framework, to hold a Chariot body. The result was called the Boston Booby.

SIX-PASSENGER ALBANY, or VIS-A-VIS
This large sleigh was often found in livery stables, and was a vehicle found in many private coach houses. It was made either with a set of long runners or a set of bob runners. A sleigh with bob runners turned much easier than other sleighs, since it had a "fifth-wheel" arrangement, like carriages do.

The use of bells was, at first, a requirement of sleighing, to warn others of an approaching turn-out. They quickly became an accepted accoutrement of sleighs and cutters, and many different forms of bells were designed, and in their more elaborate design, a mark of one's affluence.

COACHES, CARRIAGES, AND CARTS: TYPE, USE, DESIGN, AND INDUSTRY

THIS JUSTLY CELEBRATED WAGON
MANUFACTURED BY
Mitchell & Lewis Co., Limited, Racine, Wis.,

**HENRY MITCHELL
1810-1893**

Henry Mitchell, born in Fifeshire, Scotland, immigrated to America in 1834. Eventually, he set up a wagon-making business with J.V. Quarles, in Southport, Wisconsin, now called Kenosha. He sold the business to Quarles and a gentleman from New York by the name of Edward Bain. Having moved north to Racine, Wisconsin, he established a second wagon-making company, and eventually took his son-in-law, William Turner Lewis, into the company. The company was immensely successful, having 165 employees in 1871, who produced 4000 wagons. By 1882, the company was producing 16,000 wagons a year and employing 450 men. The **Mitchell Wagon** was known far and wide as an excellent farm and ranch wagon.

Wagon-making was a national industry. Many companies were renown for sturdy, serviceable wagons, many of which carried their company name on a cartouche in the lower middle panel of the side board. The John Deere and the Columbian Wagon were but two of these. The Peter Schuttler Company, of Chicago, brazenly marketed a wagon called the "Old Reliable."

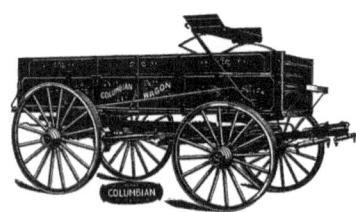

Essentially, the working part of any wagon is the gear. The front gear had an axle, hounds, bottom bolster and a ring, called the "fifth wheel." The rear part had an axle, rear hounds and a full bolster. Any type of box could be carried on the bolsters, and the reach could be lengthened to carry a longer box, if necessary.

FULL GEAR ASSEMBLED

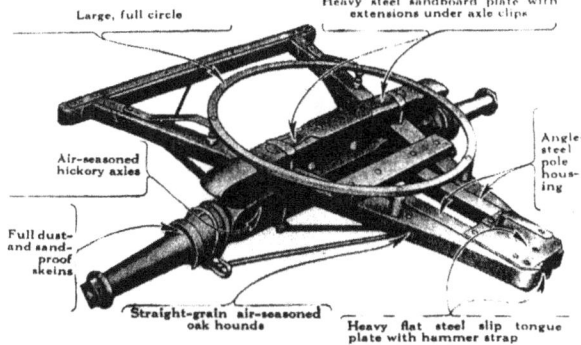

SLIP TONGUE FRONT GEAR

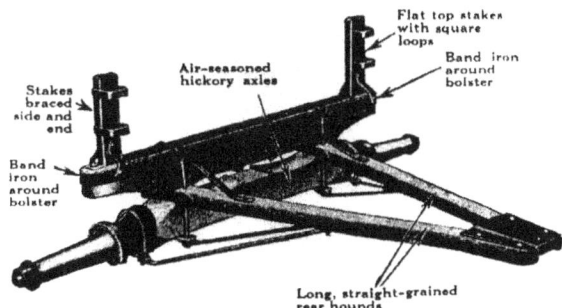

REAR GEAR

By adding a "chuck box" at the back of the wagon box, and perhaps one at the front as well, an ordinary farm wagon converted to a **Chuck Wagon**. This was the "kitchen" for many a cowboy at work on the range.

GATHERING AT THE SWEETWATER, a painting in oil by Ted Long

COACHES, CARRIAGES, AND CARTS: TYPE, USE, DESIGN, AND INDUSTRY

TROTTING RACING

Racing was a Sunday sport in most communities, and a "required" event at fair time. Every farmer hoped to have a winning horse among his stock. In buying a "road horse," it was always viewed as a possible contender.

The high neck and headset of a driving horse allows the forearm to lift at the trot. The diagonal footfalls balance the horse so breathing can be continuous for distance work. The goal is to cover 8-10 miles in one hour.

In Trotting Racing, the quest to do the mile in less than two minutes was a formidable challenge. By January of 1922, six trotters and fourteen pacers had accomplished it.

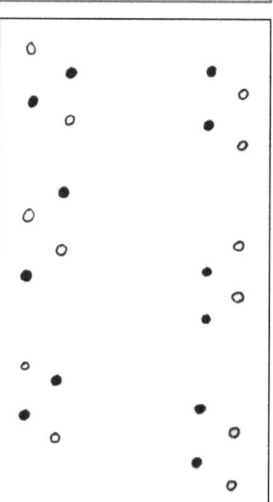

Lou Dillon was the first horse to trot the mile in less than two minutes. She made her record run at Memphis in 1903

THE TWO-MINUTE HORSE

The **trot** is a gait in which the horse moves two legs on opposite sides. It is the gait of the Carriage Horse becasue it is the most sustainable gait over a long distance. The **pace** is a gait in which the horse moves two legs on the same side. The pace is considered faster than the trot by 4 or 5 seconds.

The **Sulky** was developed as a lightweight vehicle to barely carry a driver. It is often referred to as **a skeleton cart. It used by Lou Dillon an**d was donated to the Equine Heritage Institute by Mr. Bruce Milligan of Lady Lake, FL. It is marked with the horse's name.

The **road cart**, an exercise vehicle or one intended for making fast trips to town, often served as a dual purpose vehicle, since the frugal American farmer was reluctant to buy a sulky, which could only be used for racing.

As the bicycle tire came into vogue, it was quickly adapted to the sulky. In the early days it was the cause of accidents, when the balloon tire exploded and frightened the animal. The familiar hooped-shaped body better accommodated the wheel arch necessary to hold a spoke wheel and tire.

The four-wheel sulky, thought by some to give greater stability, appeared almost at the same time as the two-wheel sulky. In its balloon-tire form, it was called a **matinee wagon**.

THE FINAL MILE

O Mighty Monarchs of the Equine Race,
    Just when will come the zenith of your flight?
What voice will guide your flying feet apace,
    And prompt you in your crowning trial aright?
What deft and clever wizard of the reins
    Will urge you onward with uncanny hand?
What blood will course within your royal veins,
    And who will view your triumphs from the stand?
What of the track and where the test?
    When will you reach the dizzy heights sublime?
What starting judge will find you at your best,
    And where will stop the second hand of time?

This much I know, your freedom's near
    From toil and hardship that has long been yours,
And to supplant them there will soon appear
    The rare devotion that so long endures.
And you, divorced from baser parts,
    From war, and strife, and greed and pelf,
Will be enshrined within the hearts
    That love you for yourself.
And when that roseate day shall fall
    And all is ready for the final mile,
I know the Great Presiding Judge of all
    Will look down from those pearly gates and smile.

—*Walter Palmer.*

Sept. 1909 edition of the Horse Review, Fred Ernst drives Baron Alcyon to victory at Readville Trotting Park.

THE KLADRUBER

The Chariot of Franz Joseph I, made by Carl Marius of Vienna, emerges from the Michael Trakt of the Hofburg in Vienna. Eight Kladrubers, in State harness, are pulling this carriage, now exhibited at the Wagenburg.

The Emperor Maximilian II, 1552-1612, Founder of the stud at Kladruby nad Labem, inherited the domain of Pardubice. It included the village and game park of Kladruby, where he kept unusual horses. The Emperor Rudolf II, an eccentric individual prizing his privacy more than anything else, established a court stud at Kladruby nad Labem in 1579.

The black Kladuber was founded by two stallions with the same name. The line of one of them. Sacramoso foaled in 1800, lives on today. One of the saddest days in the history of this line, was in 1930, when most of the black horses were sold for meat. Later, regretting such a move, successful attempts were made to regenerate the line.

The white Kladruber is still bred at the Kladruby stud, tracing its line to a Spanish-Italian stallion named Peppoli, foaled in 1764.

Symbol	Name	Symbol	Name
G ⌒	Generale	A ⟨⟩	Alarm
⌒ ♠	Generalissimus	Dk	Diktant
F ☐	Favory	Se	Servator
S ✠	Sacramoso	Mk ⌂	Mykonos
Ru ⌒	Rudolfo	Q ⊗	Quoniam
F Ⱶ	Furioso	Z ✦	North Star
P △	Przedswit	⌒ ⌽	Solo

On the left side, there is a brand which identifies its sire and sire of his dam.

Rudolfo, the off wheeler at Continental Acres is marked:

Ru I   His sire is Rudolfo I
☐   The sire of his dam is Favory IX

On the right side is a number, which indicates which foal of his sire he is.

6   He is the sixth son of Rudolfo I

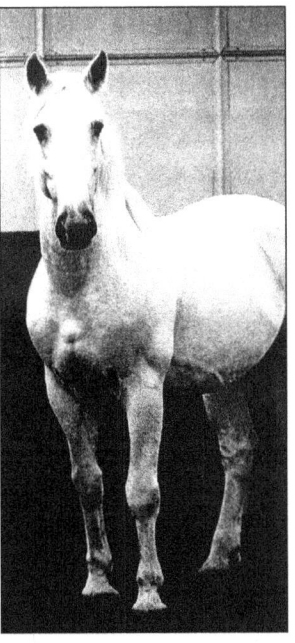
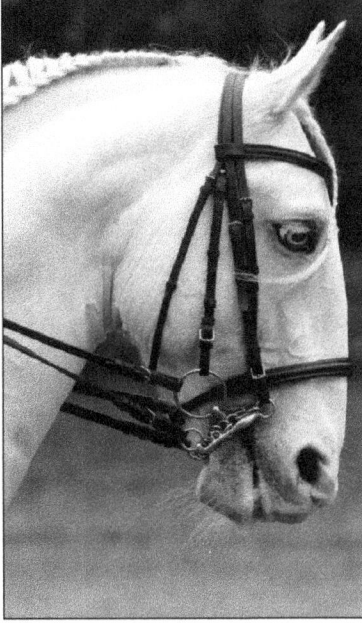

Place of origin: Czechoslovakia (Bohemia)
Height at withers: 16.2-17 hands
Structure: mesomorphic
Colour: grey—black
Temperament: calm but lively
Aptitude: light draught—fast heavy draught—saddle horse
Qualities: strong and generous
Head: elongated—profile convex—forehead broad—eyes large—nostrils wide—jaws pronounced
Neck: well proportioned—muscular—slightly arched
Body: withers broad and not very pronounced—back long and straight—loins full—quarters short and broad, rounded—tail well set-on, flowing and fine—chest full and deep
Legs: strong—well muscled—shoulder nicely sloping and muscular—forearm and leg quite long—knee and hock broad and clean—cannons slender but solid—tendons strong, clearly defined and set well apart—pasterns rather long—feet well shaped with tough horn on the hoof

The **Kladruber horse**, having old Spanish and Italian blood, shares a common ancestry with the Lipizzan. It is the national horse of the Czech Republic. It was used as a majestic ceremonial horse by the imperial Court in Vienna.

Scaramuie, a horse ridden by Emperor Karl VI being led by a trainer. The mane is plaited. The painting is by Johann Georg von Hamilton, c. 1720.

COACHES, CARRIAGES, AND CARTS: TYPE, USE, DESIGN, AND INDUSTRY

THE MORGAN

Place of origin: United States
Height at withers: 14.2-15.3 hands
Weight: 880-1,100 lb (400-500 kg)
Structure: mesomorphic
Colour: bay—chestnut—black; white markings common
Temperament: docile but energetic
Aptitude: harness and saddle horse
Qualities: fast and with good stamina—versatile
Head: of average size and slightly tapering from the jaw to the muzzle—profile straight—ears small and pointed—eyes set well apart and expressive—nostrils broad
Neck: of average length and muscular—arched—mane thick
Body: withers well defined but not too high—back short and wide—loins strong—croup rather long and rounded—tail well set-on and full—chest broad and muscular—girth deep
Legs: sturdy and muscular—shoulder long, sloping and muscular—well-developed bone structure and joints—forearm long and muscular—cannons short—tendons well defined—pasterns of medium length and not too sloping—hoof well formed, of average size and good thickness.

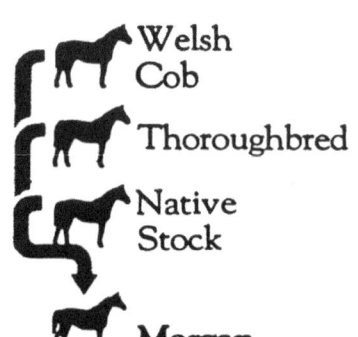

The **Morgan** is the only breed founded by a single stallion and the only breed named for its foundation sire.

Justin Morgan was foaled in 1789, in Massachusetts. He was sired by True Briton, a Thoroughbred. His Dam is unknown, but thought to be part Arab, or Barb and some cold blood.

Three stallions sired by Justin Morgan, became the foundation Stock; Bulrush, Woodbury and Sherman. Sherman was the sire of Black Hawk, who produced the renown Ethan Allen.

Among the many uses of the Morgan horse, his natural ability to draw great weight made him an ideal driving horse.

This pair, Parade and Broadwall Drum Major, has been a consistent winner for their owners, Mr. and Mrs. J. Cecil Ferguson of Broadwall Farm, Green RI. They led the revival of carriage driving among Morgan owners and were early supporters of the Carriage Association of America.

The statue of Justin Morgan at The Morgan Horse Farm, Weybridge, Vermont. This farm, was originally owned by Joseph Battell, the man responsible for compiling the Morgan Register.

REX'S MAJOR MONTE
This horse bears an uncanny resemblance to Justin Morgan and typifies the breed characteristics.

BROADWALL DRUM MAJOR
Broadwall Farm, Green, RI

WINDCREST DONFIELD
Waseeka Farm, Ashland, MA

COACHES, CARRIAGES, AND CARTS: TYPE, USE, DESIGN, AND INDUSTRY

THE BRIDLE

A bridle is used to drive the horse. It is usually blinker bridle, as the Blinkers protect the eyes, especially in multiples.

A bridle consists of:
- Crown piece
- Blinker
- Browband
- Noseband
- Face drop
- Bearing rein
- Throat latch
- Cheek strap

THE LIVERPOOL BIT

This is the most widely accepted of all curb bits. The cheeks can be fixed or swivel, and a variety of mouthpieces can be used with it. It allows for several positions for the reins.

1 - the Plain Cheek, and most common position
2 - the Rough Cheek
3 - the Middle Bar
4 - the Bottom Bar

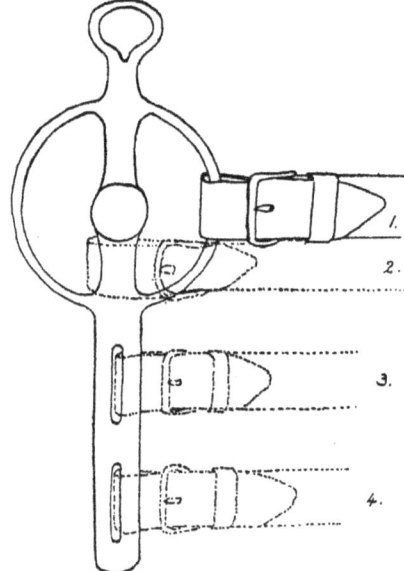

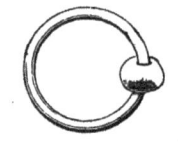
Plain Ring.

Ring with Barrel Brace.

Double or Four Ring.

Double Ring with Double Mouth-Piece.

66 COACHES, CARRIAGES, AND CARTS: TYPE, USE, DESIGN, AND INDUSTRY

DIFFERENT MOUTHPIECES WHICH CAN BE MOUNTED IN DIFFERENT BITS.

Horses differed greatly in their ability to take a bit. Some horses required a more severe bit than others.

A pair of coach horses in formal harness. The bridles are fitted with buxton bits and bearing reins.

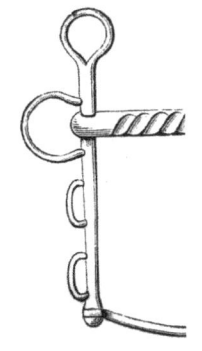

- Straight Bar.
- Mullen.
- Jointed.
- Twisted.
- Half Rough.
- Rollers.
- Double.

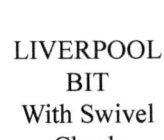

- Double and Twisted.
- Cambridge.
- Melton.
- Full Port.
- Greenwood.
- Chain.

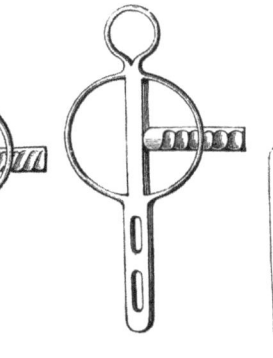

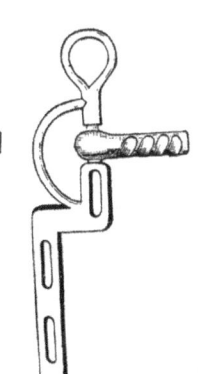

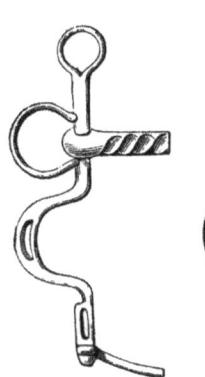

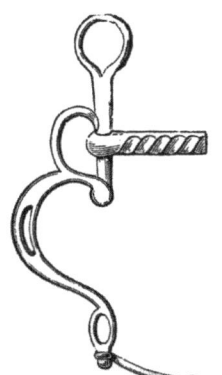

| GIG BIT
With bar | LIVERPOOL BIT
With Swivel Cheek | LIVERPOOL BIT | ELBOW BIT
With Swivel Cheek | ASHLEIGH BIT
Extra hole for a billet strap in the upper shank | BUXTON BIT
The most formal of driving bits | FANCY BUXTON |

COACHES, CARRIAGES, AND CARTS: TYPE, USE, DESIGN, AND INDUSTRY

THE DRIVING BIT

A driving bit is marked by two characteristics. In the first place it has more than one placement for the rein; in the second place, it always has a **Snaffle Position** for the rein (which is just a direct pull.). Usually, the reins are attached to slots in the lower shanks to activate the curb or lever action, which applies pressure to the mouth, chin groove, and pole. There are several types, the most common being a curb bit.

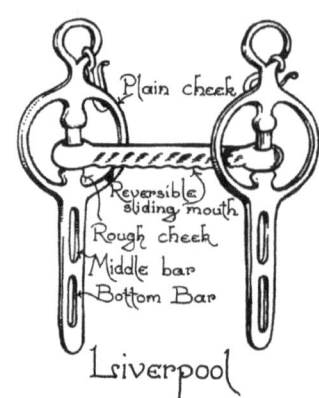

THE SNAFFLE BIT

The **Hungarian** or **Wilson Snaffle**, with a jointed mouthpiece is an acceptable driving bit. It is the most common type of bit used. It consists of a bit mouthpiece with a ring on either side and acts with direct pressure. The snaffle bit works on several parts of the horse's mouth.

THE CURB BIT

The curb bit has several parts: two cheek pieces, a mouthpiece and two hooks for the chin chain.

This driving bit has three points of action. It can exert **poll pressure**, or mouth pressure, or chin pressure.

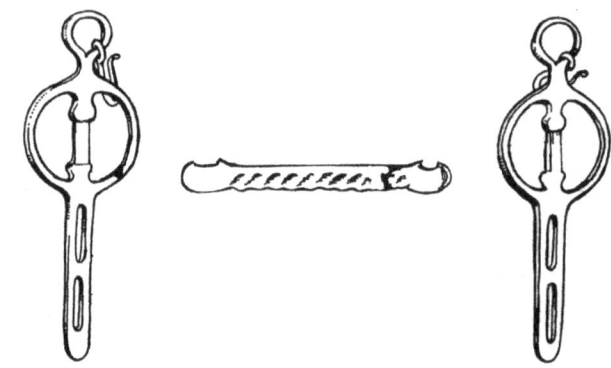

CHIN PRESSURE

A chain, running beneath the chin lies in a groove behind the lower lip. The curb chain exerts pressure on the mandible nerve, a large, very sensitive nerve running along the edge of the lower jaw.

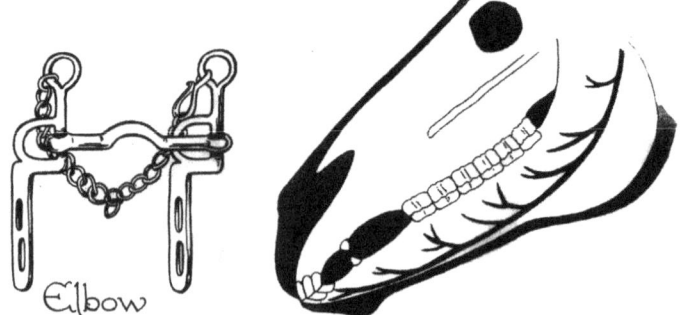

68 COACHES, CARRIAGES, AND CARTS: TYPE, USE, DESIGN, AND INDUSTRY

POLL PRESSURE

Pressure is exerted on the poll by using the mouthpiece as a fulcrum to pull on the cheek straps and headband.

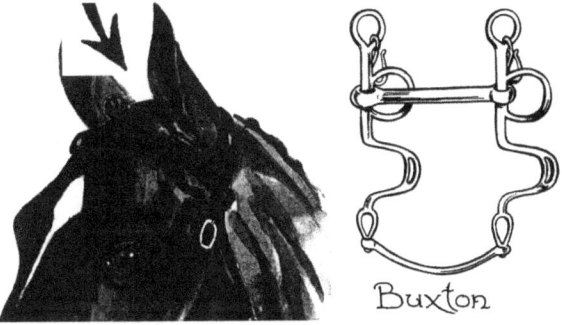

MOUTH AND TONGUE PRESSURE

A mouthpiece lies on the BARS of the mouth, a gum area between the incisors in front and the molars at the back of the mouth. Exerting steady pressure on the bars will force a horse to lower its head.

Various types of mouthpieces have been designed to effect different action on the bars and achieve a designated result.

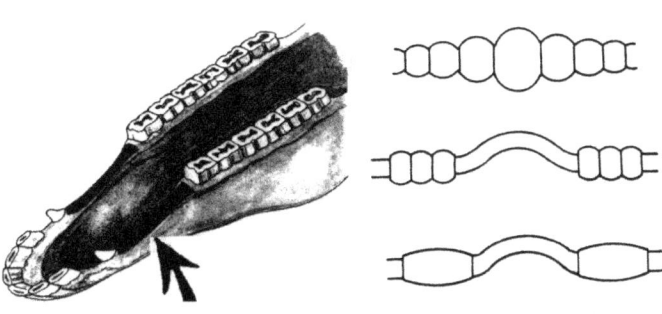

SWALES

The **swales bit** is a unique driving bit, which exerts no poll pressure.

medium-port Liverpool Swales

Barmouth with bottom bar Swales

medium-port Swales

A **Port** in the mouthpiece accommodates the horse's tongue, when a straight bar mouthpiece proves unaccommodating to the horse.

SEGUNDO PORT

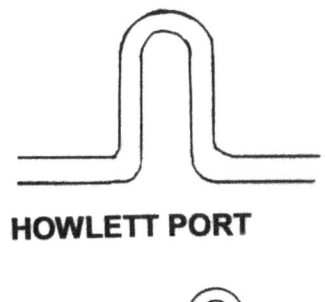
HOWLETT PORT

MEDIUM PORT

LOW PORT

THE BEARING REIN

Bearing reins were used in the 1800's to elevate a carriage horse's head. These reins were uncomfortable and even painful for horses and were abolished partially in part to the protest raised by Anna Sewell's novel Black Beauty.

A bearing rein is intended to prevent the horse from grazing, losing its bridle, or getting the bridle or bit caught on the carriage pole or harness on the other horse. A form of bearing rein is used today, but is a much more humane device. Today most horse harnesses include an overcheck or sidecheck, which are comparable to a bearing rein but are adjusted more humanely. An overcheck helps a horse maintain their balance and gives a handler more control. An overcheck does not force the horse's head up painfully, but is usually set at the horse's optimal natural carriage. (cited. http://www.luckypony.com/articles/horse_bearing_reins.htm)

They're most often seen on Hackneys and other horses with naturally high head carriages. Some believe they help prevent the reins from being caught in the shafts but if they're holding the horse's head that high, they're probably too tight.

The direct bearing rein attaches to the bridoon, runs through a drop ring at the sides of the horse's bridle and attaches to the hook on the back pad (harness saddle).

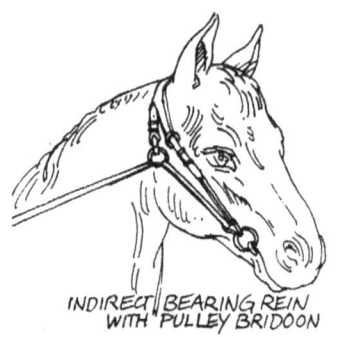

INDIRECT BEARING REIN WITH PULLEY BRIDOON

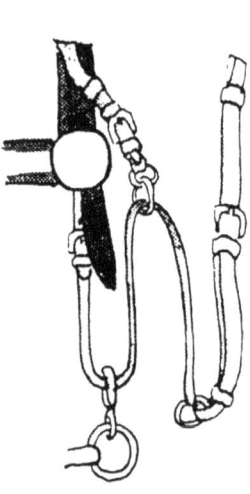

The indirect bearing rein attaches to a small strap, called a point, on the crown piece, at the sides of the bridle. It passes through a small pulley on the bridoon, and then passes trough the drop and then attaches to the hook on the back pad of the harness.

When the driving bit does not have a jointed mouthpiece, one should use a jointed bridoon.

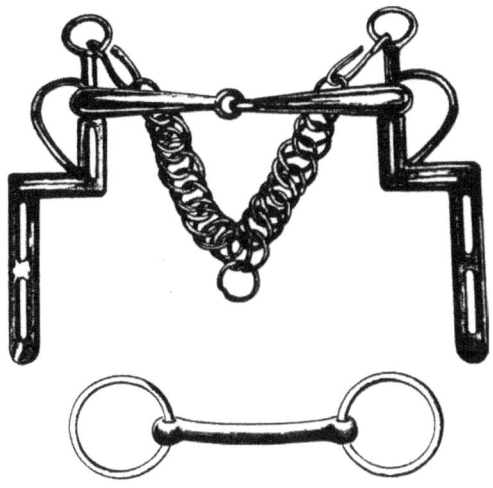

When using a jointed, half-cheek (spoon snaffle), the use of an overcheck, with a unjointed bridoon, was popular for road racing. This type of bitting is still used in the show ring today and for track racing.

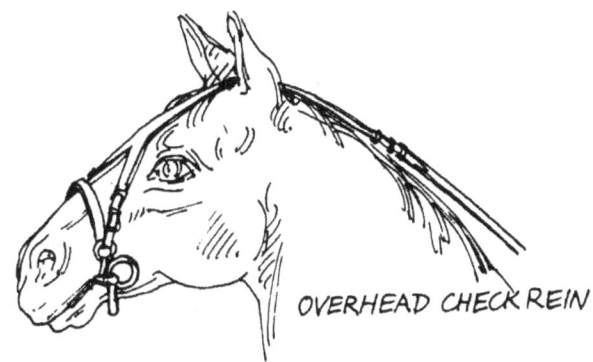

OVERHEAD CHECK REIN

When the mouthpiece of the driving bit is jointed, one should use an unjointed bridoon.

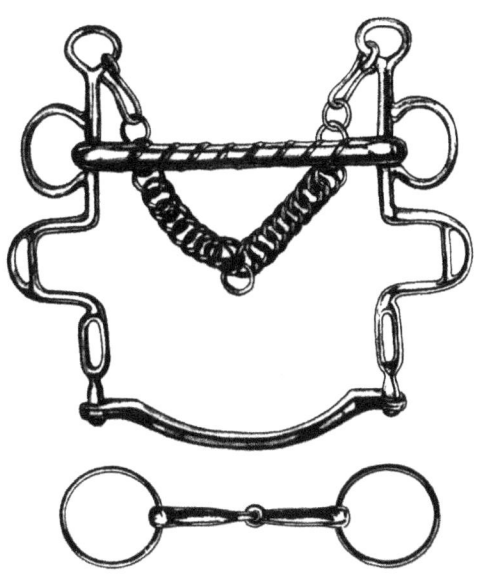

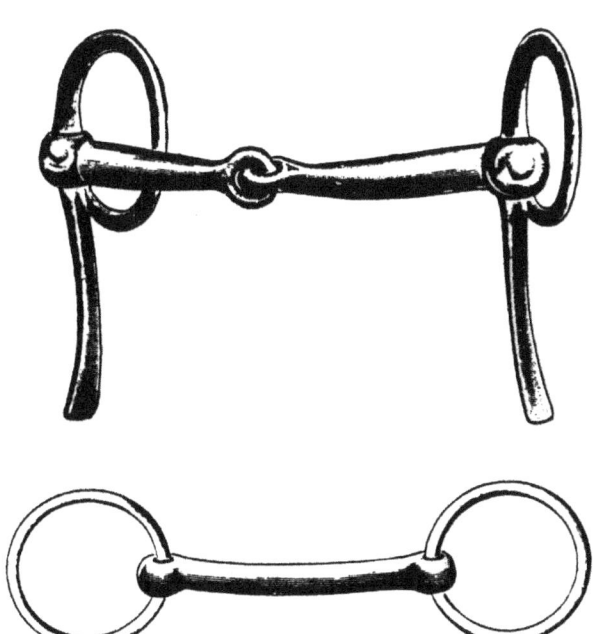

COACHES, CARRIAGES, AND CARTS: TYPE, USE, DESIGN, AND INDUSTRY

EVOLUTION OF THE HARNESS

It is widely believed the horse was first harnessed in Kazakhstan, from there the technology quickly spread to what is now Europe. Early harness was completely different than what we see today. They were poorly designed and often placed the weight of the load across the horses wind pipe in a neck/girth system. The first change was a strap harness, with a "chest" strap pulling the load. This and new advances in chariot-making made horse drawn warfare and travel easier. However the horse harnesses were still not able to pull very heavy loads or loads being dragged on the ground. The answer to this dilemma was discovered in China. The horse collar was developed, this allowed for horses to pull heavier loads. The collar rested on the horses shoulders and chest and prevented the horse from choking. These two "updated" harnesses are not far from what we all are used to seeing today. (cited. http://www.saddleonline.com/blogs/content/history-harness)

The Classical Harness,/ Neck and Girth Harness (top) was the type used with light-weight chariots. It was adapted from the type of harness used on oxen and not suited to the horse's anatomy.

The Breast-strap Harness/ Breast Collar (middle) which originated in China first appeared 480-221 BCE. It did not appear in Europe until the 500's CE.

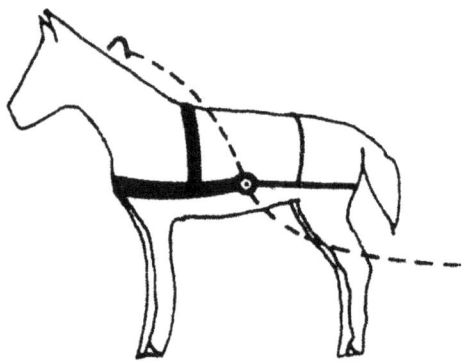

Medieval Harness/ Full Collar Harness (bottom) originated in China in about 100 BCE and did not appear in Europe until the 700's CE. It was revolutionary and specifically designed for the horse. (cited from the work of Joseph Needham)

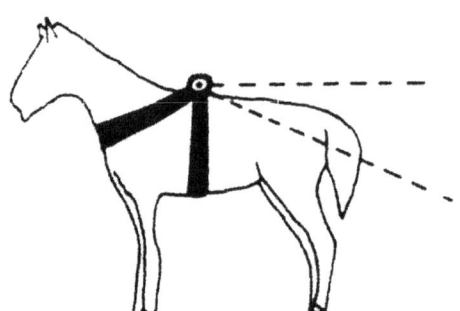

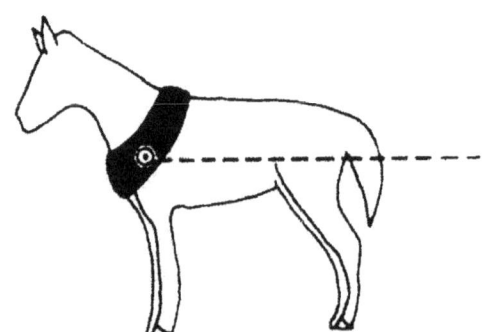

YOKE AS USED WITH THE HORSE

GREECE

End of pole, with elaborate Cross bar or Yoke.

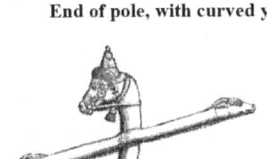
End of pole, with curved yoke.

Assyrian chariot containing

End of pole, with cross-bar,

ASSYRIA

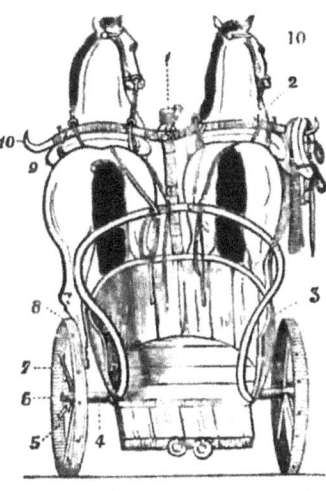

1. ῥυμός. 2. οἴηξ. 3. δίφρος. 4. ἄξων. 5. ἴτυς. 6. πλήμνη. 7. κνήμη. 8. ἐπίσσωτρα. 9. ζεύγλη. 10. ζυγόν.

CHARIOT NECK AND GIRTH HARNESS

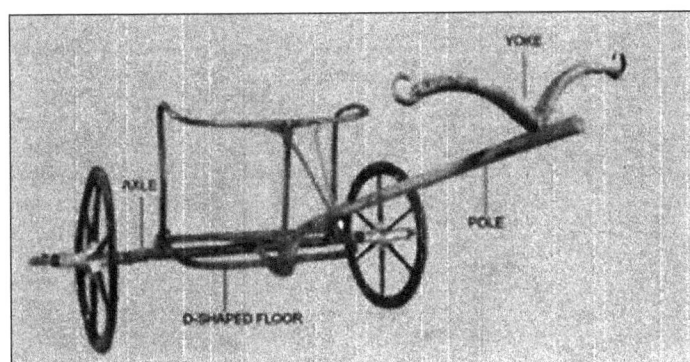

EGYPT

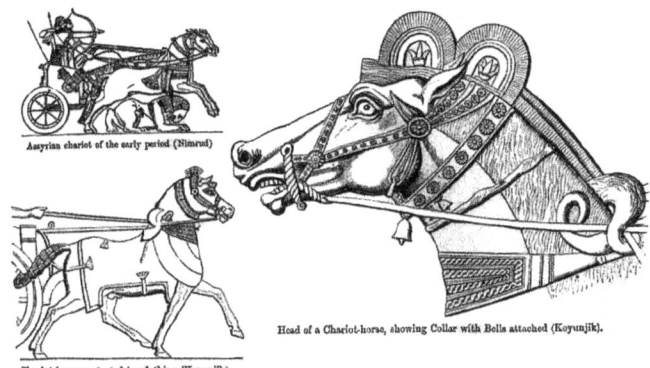

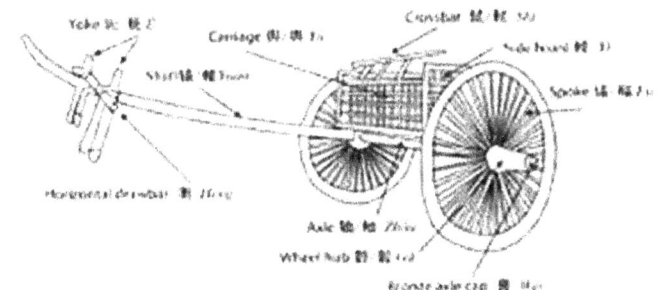

CHINA

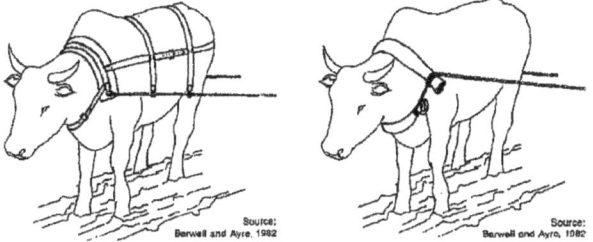

Source: Barwell and Ayre, 1982

COACHES, CARRIAGES, AND CARTS: TYPE, USE, DESIGN, AND INDUSTRY

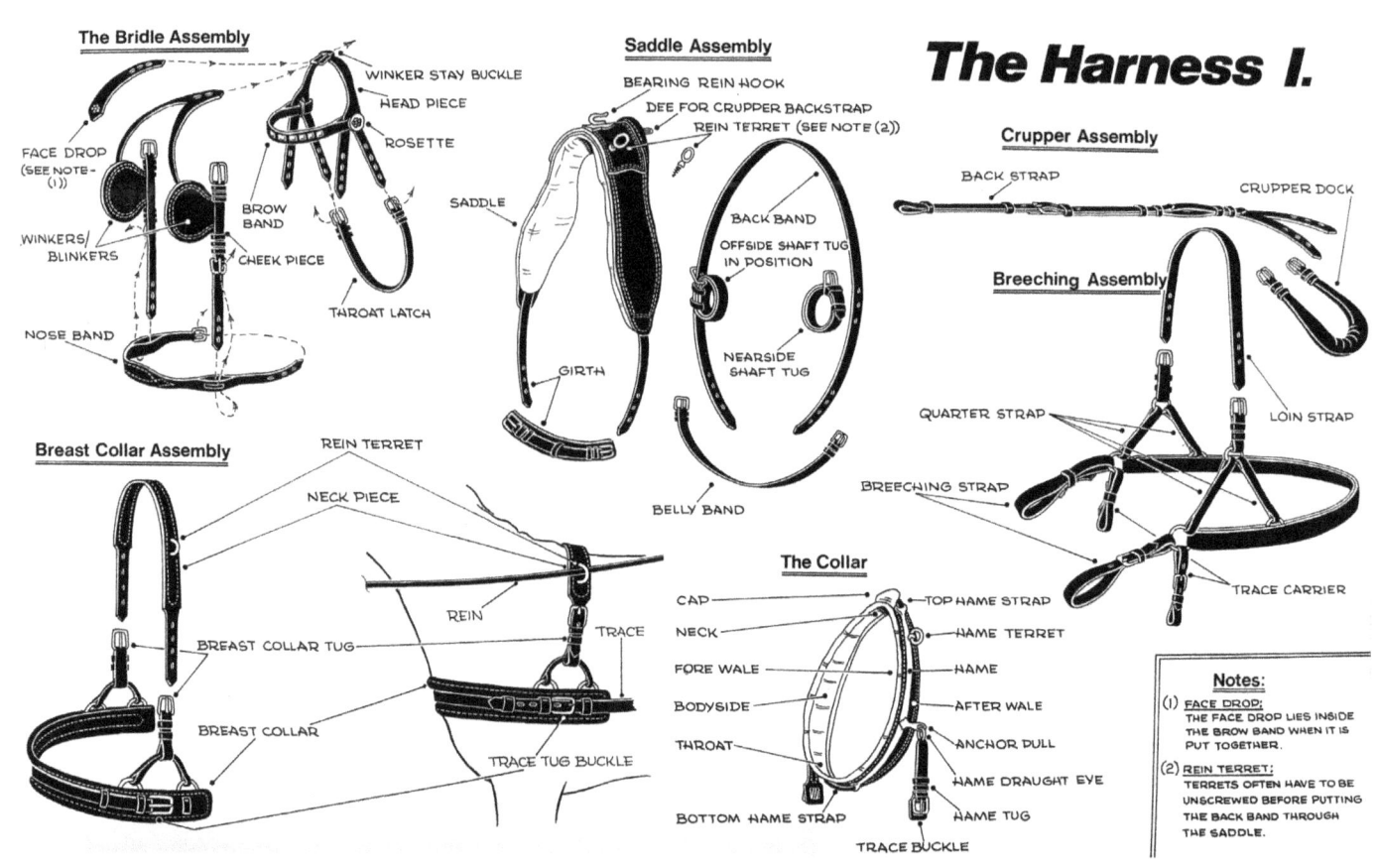

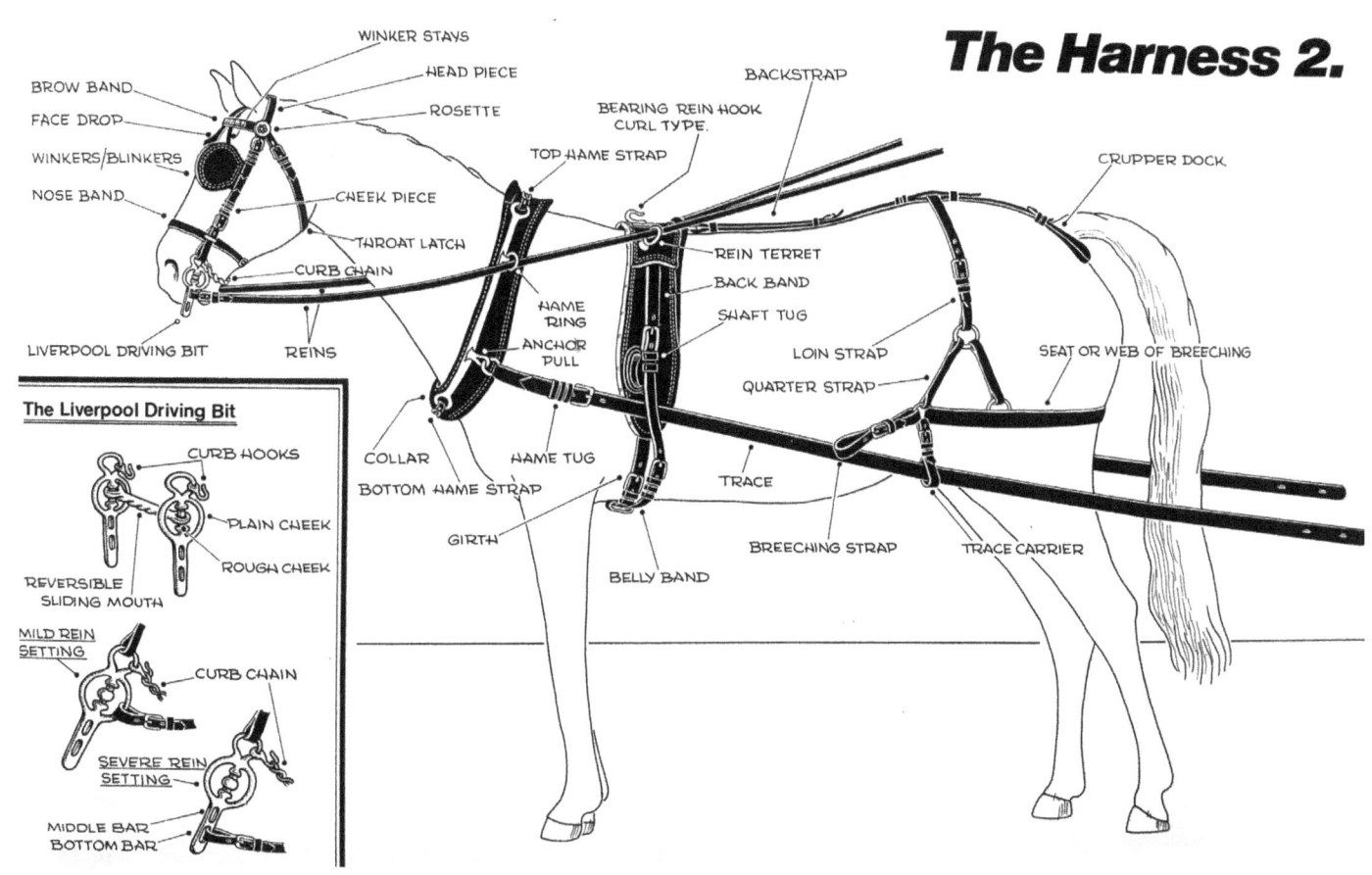

COACHES, CARRIAGES, AND CARTS: TYPE, USE, DESIGN, AND INDUSTRY 75

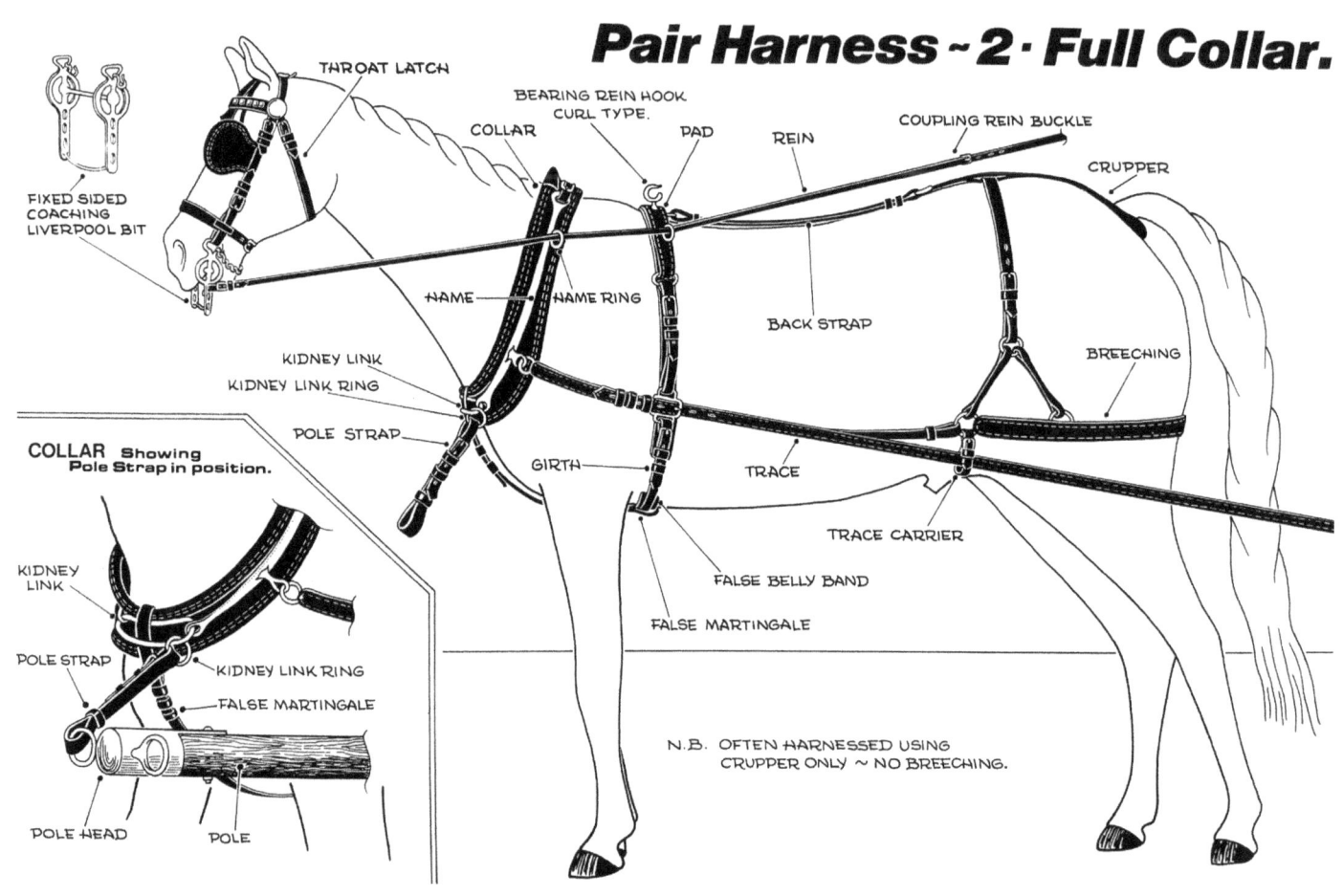

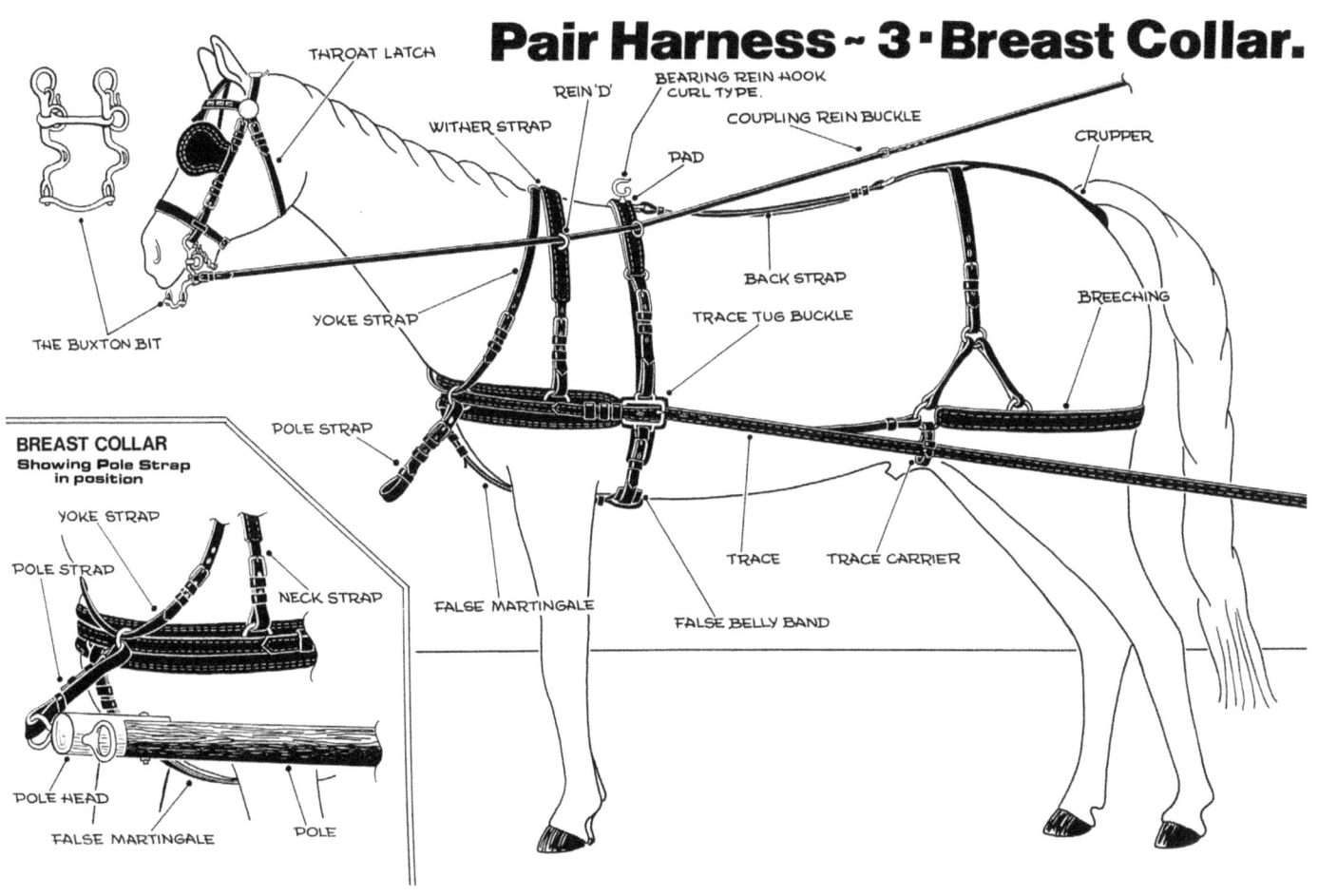

COACHES, CARRIAGES, AND CARTS: TYPE, USE, DESIGN, AND INDUSTRY 77

DRIVING

The art of tooling a carriage around the park in fashionable style required some practice. There were accepted ways to hold the reins. In driving a single horse or a pair, both reins were held in the left hand, clamped by the third and fourth fingers. One rein (the left) was placed over the index finger; the second rein (the right) was placed between the second and third fingers. The right hand was used to drive as needed, or as comfortable, and also held the whip.

A carriage driver wore driving gloves, usually made of dog skin. Some gloves were reinforced in the proper places for the reins. The driver also carried a whip, which became the singular badge of the "coachman." The driver became fashionably known as the **"The Whip."**

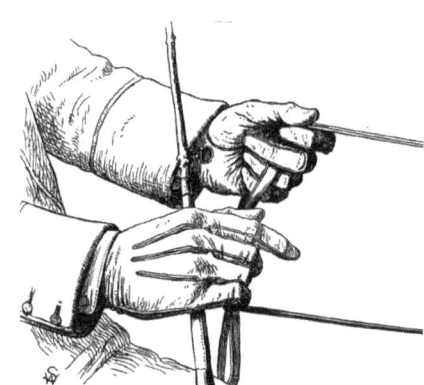

THE FULL HAND METHOD OF HOLDING FOUR REINS When one wished to drive four horses, the left lead rein replaced the single left rein on top of the index finger. The right wheel rein replaced the single right rein. The right lead rein was placed on top of the left wheel rein and both were then placed between the index finger and the second finger.

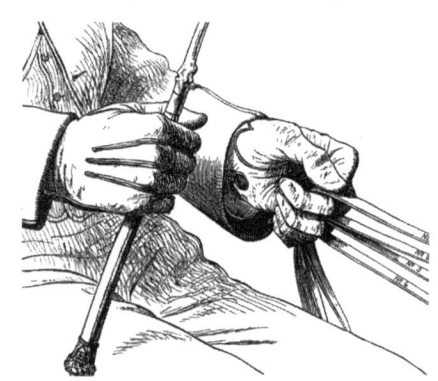

Skeleton Break, used to train and exercise four-in-hands.

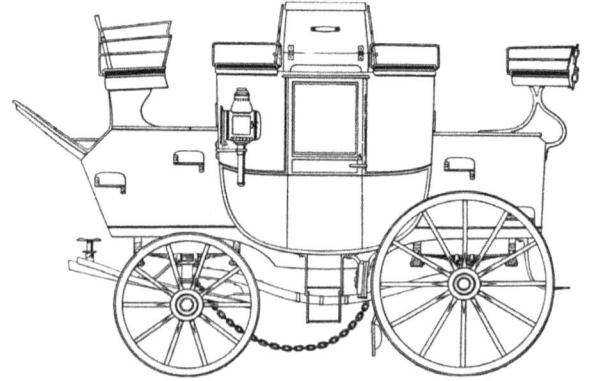

Park Drag, a Gentleman's Private Coach

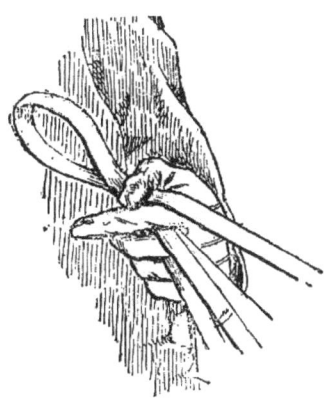

The top or near leader rein is looped under the thumb of the left hand to commence the leaders to turn left.

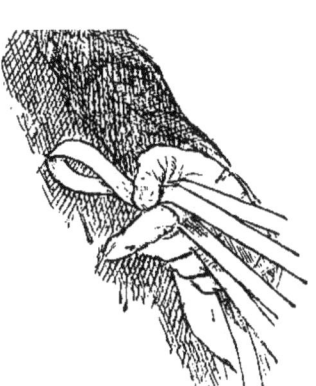

The off leader rein is looped under the thumb in the left hand to commence the leaders to turn right.

When the horse or horses are bent in the direction of the turn, the right hand is placed on the reins to the inside or outside of the turn to signal lateral movements either to the right or left. This allows the whip to direct the footfalls of each set of horses to move through gateways and around corners.

Clubbing the reins is the procedure of placing all reins in the left hand by placing the off reins on top of the hand with the index finger separating the off reins.

Point to the Left

Point to the Right

Point to the Left

Point to the Right

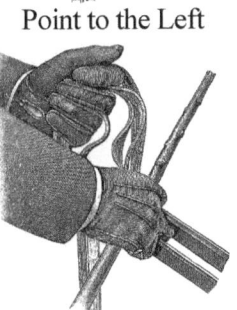

Stopping

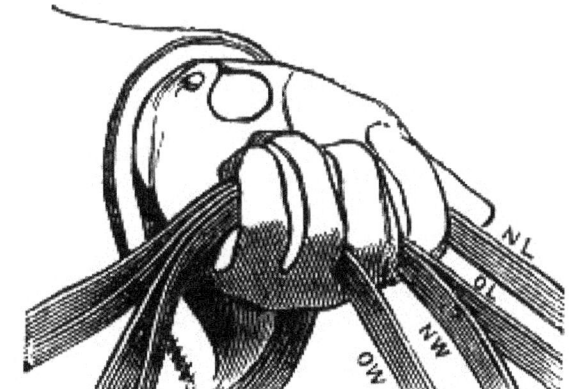

Close-up of reins for four-in-hand driving

COACHES, CARRIAGES, AND CARTS: TYPE, USE, DESIGN, AND INDUSTRY

NATIONAL REINING STYLES

In the English method, the near lead rein is held over the fore-finger of the left hand. The off lead rein and the near wheel rein are held between the first and second fingers, the lead rein on top; the off wheel rein is held between the second and third fingers.

There are several different methods of holding reins and driving, mostly used in the country of origin.

In France, the **Full Hand** method is used, one rein over the fore-finger and one between each successive finger.

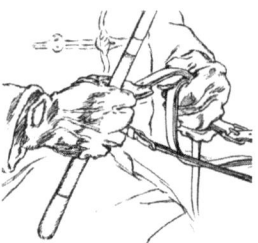

The Hungarian method employs a **brezel**, i.e. a hand piece to which all reins are coupled. Although there are several ways by which reins may be coupled to it, each rein eventually couples back to this single hand piece.

The drivers of the Swiss and Italian Diligences, use a wide variety of methods. In all, the near lead-rein and the near wheel or the off lead rein are held over the fore-finger. Sometimes both off lead-rein and wheel-rein are held between the first and second fingers; at other times the near wheel-rein is held between the first and second fingers and the off wheel-rein between the second and third fingers.

In Russia, both reins to each horse are held in the respective left or right hand. When driving a **Troika**, there is only an outside rein to the galloping horses, a check rein being used to hook them to the trotting horse in the center. The driver holds his arms outstretched in front of himself.

In America, the stage-driver holds the near lead rein on top and the near wheel-rein beneath the fourth finger of the left hand. He holds the off lead-rein on top and the off wheel-rein beneath the second finger of the right hand.

When the driver wishes to hold the reins altogether in his left hand, he merely shifts those from his right hand to the corresponding position in his left hand. This is called **clubbing**.

COACHES, CARRIAGES, AND CARTS: TYPE, USE, DESIGN, AND INDUSTRY

WHIPS

The whip is the distinguishing badge of the coachman, or driver. A knowledge of its proper use is **de rigeur,** and no driver is excused from the need to know how to use a whip properly.

The correct driving whip consists of a length of holly wood, or some other wood, with a leathered handle, delicately ferruled, to which a bow top and lash are attached. The bow top is made of a bit of whalebone and/or goose quills, and must be hung properly when not in use, just to preserve its shape.

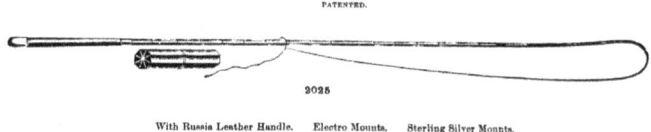

BUILT CANE DRIVING WHIP.

PATENTED.

2025

With Russia Leather Handle.   Electro Mounts.   Sterling Silver Mounts.

Different kinds of wooden sticks were used, and many styles of handles, much to the owner's preference. Whatever the design, the second ferrule was an important marker.

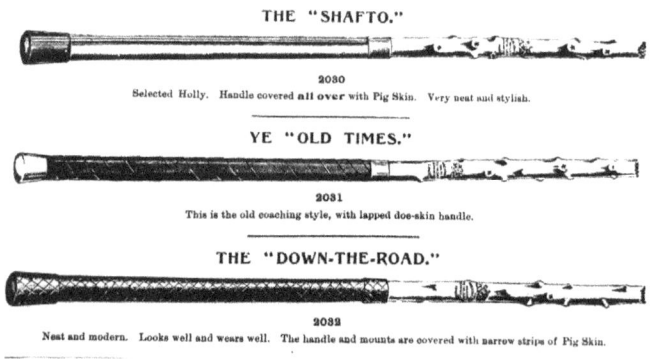

THE "SHAFTO."

2030
Selected Holly. Handle covered all over with Pig Skin. Very neat and stylish.

YE "OLD TIMES."

2031
This is the old coaching style, with lapped doe-skin handle.

THE "DOWN-THE-ROAD."

2032
Neat and modern. Looks well and wears well. The handle and mounts are covered with narrow strips of Pig Skin.

- The English use a bow whip that has a quill braided into the leather lash at the end of the stick.

- A buggy whip, which was seen in America, has a very short lash.

- The Hungarians use what is called a "drop thong" whip.

- The whip lash has to be long enough to reach the shoulder(s) of the horse(s) in single or pair and long enough to reach the shoulder of the lead horse(s) when driving more.

The proper form for driving a single horse or a pair is to hold the whip in the right hand, balancing it as close to the second ferrule as convenient. The reins are held in the left hand, while both hands are used to drive.

Learning the use of a four-in-hand whip required much practice in dropping the thong properly. Such a whip is never carried with the lash extended, as the whip for pairs or singles.

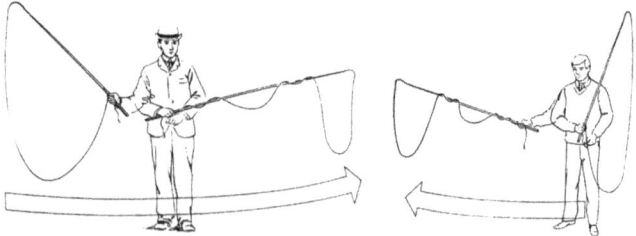

82 COACHES, CARRIAGES, AND CARTS: TYPE, USE, DESIGN, AND INDUSTRY

TOUCHING THE HORSE

In order to signal the horse in performing some of the lateral movements required in driving dressage, the horse can be touched with the bow top, or stroked with the lash, behind the pad, in places to which the horse has been accustomed to receive a cue.

STRIKING THE HORSE

If one chooses to hit the horse, it should be done quickly, decisively and accurately. Such a strike is always in front of the pad, never behind it. In no circumstance is a driver expected to whip the horse.

SIGNALS

The whip is a driving aid, and also an implement to signal other drivers. Turning is indicated by the whip.

Greetings are also conveyed with the whip: To a colleague, a raised elbow, with the whip still held across the breast is customary.

A formal salute, used by members of the coaching club, when passing in parade before the President, held the whip across the face.

At other times, the whip held perpendicular before the face is considered the best form.

COACHES, CARRIAGES, AND CARTS: TYPE, USE, DESIGN, AND INDUSTRY

TANDEM

Driving tandem offered the opportunity of handling four reins, but only controlling two horses. considered the most difficult of all driving, it took great skill to keep the leader working well, since it had no companion to help it or work with it.

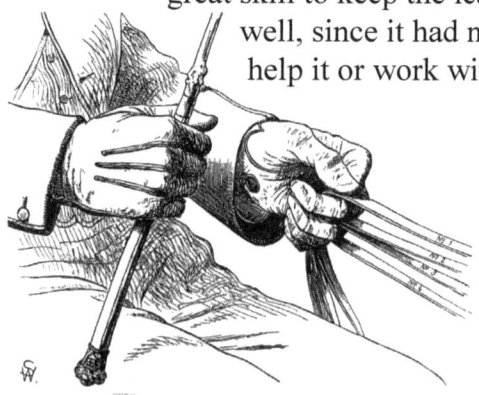

Tandem driving began when a would-be fox hunter drove his hunter to a Dog Cart, carrying himself, his friends and his hounds to the hunt. Finding his hunter too worn out from his exertions to hunt well, he used a Cob to pull his turnout and attached the hunter in front, to trot to the hunt without doing much work.

TANDEM HARNESS

A special two-wheel vehicle was reserved for this particular sport, the Tandem Cart. Often, it was nothing more than a large Village Cart of Ralli Car that had been equipped to drive tandem. Gradually, larger Dog Carts were used, and these were specifically named Tandem Carts.

In the first, the lead horse is attached to the turnout by two traces, which are coupled to a prong built out from the trace buckle on the wheeler's harness.

In the second, the leader's traces are shorter, and are attached to hooks on a bar, which is hung from a second bar hung from the wheeler's collar.

TANDEM DETAILS

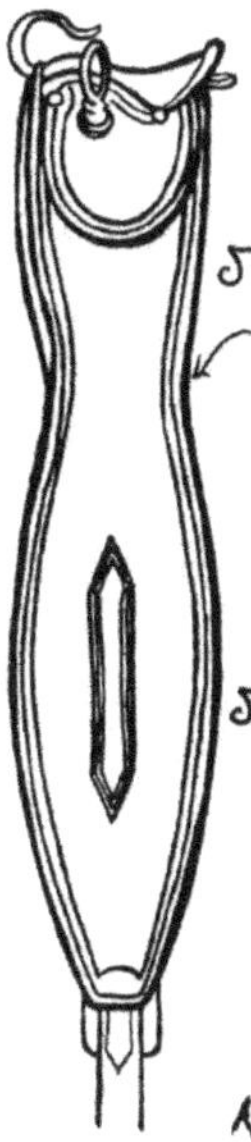

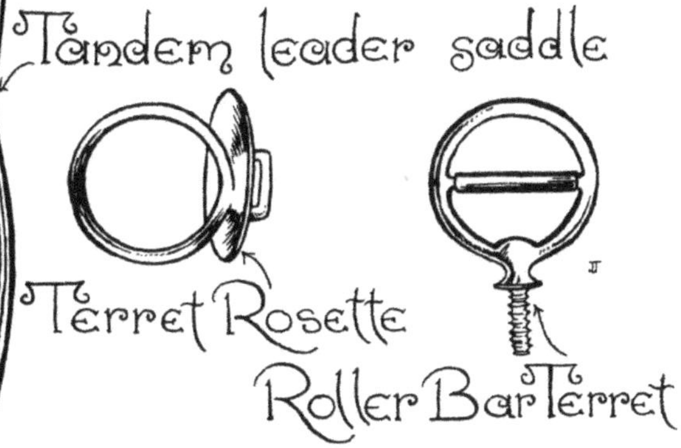

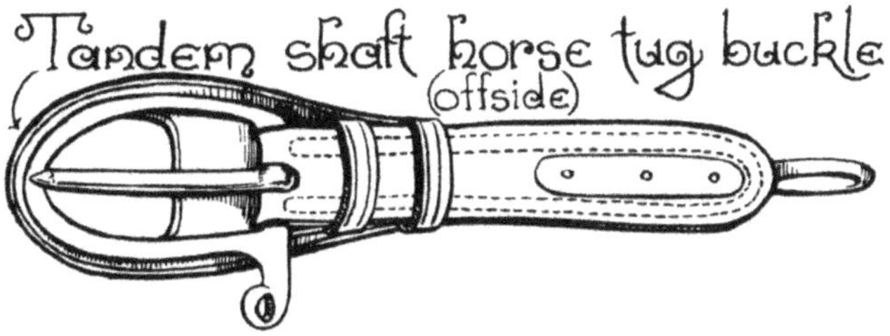

- Tandem leader saddle
- Terret Rosette
- Roller Bar Terret
- Spring cockeye
- Tandem shaft horse tug buckle (offside)
- Tandem Bars

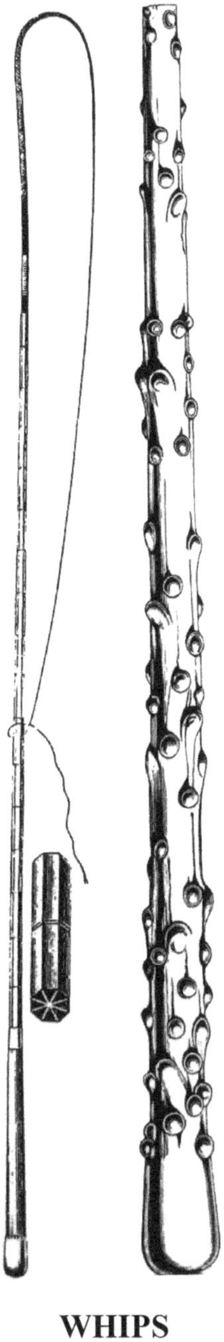

Custom and usage has developed two types of tandem harness.

The driver, known as the whip, was expected to wear gloves, hat, carry a driving whip and cover his clothes with a driving rug. The driving whip was usually made of holly, because it had nodules which would permit the driver to furl the lash around it and out of harm's way until needed.

DRIVING GLOVES

WHIPS

COACHES, CARRIAGES, AND CARTS: TYPE, USE, DESIGN, AND INDUSTRY

POSTILION DRIVING

Long distance traveling through England and on the continent was done in rented carriages or privately owned vehicles. The traveler hired riders, or postilions, to drive horses rented at inns and livery stables along the route. One postilion, who was in charge of the turn-out, rode the near (left) wheeler; a second postilion rode the near leader.

The near wheeler horse, on which the postilion rider is mounted, was called the **Ride Horse**; the off horse was called the **Hand Horse**. It is "led" by a single rein, which has a small ring at the end. This ring runs on a small strap, which is attached to the sides of the bit. The post boy rode the near wheeler horse and led the off horse, guiding it with the postilion whip held in his right hand. There are instances known, where one postilion on the near wheel horse drove two, and sometimes, three, leaders. Known as post "boys", these riders were sometimes as old as sixty-five. They enjoyed the travelers' confidence and were of good moral character and abstemious habits.

(Above) A team of Windsor Greys, harnessed "a la grand daumont," with silver mane dressings, are leaving the Royal Mews (London) on the occasion of the marriage of Prince Andrew, the Duke of York, to Miss Sarah Ferguson. The postilions are wearing Ascot livery. The carriage is the 1902 Postilion Landau.

86 COACHES, CARRIAGES, AND CARTS: TYPE, USE, DESIGN, AND INDUSTRY

Attelage De Poste - Plate XVIII from Lene, Sellerie Francais, Paris, 1878. This turn out was used for long distance posting, but when the turn out became the very fashionable "a la grand daumont" style of driving, the horses were harnessed with lighter saddles and collars.

Since the riders were called "postilions," the system was called **posting**. Gradually,  large numbers of second-hand Chariots were made available for rent. They were most often painted yellow, and were referred to as Yellow Bounders. The print above, taken from a painting by James Pollard, entitled "The last hour of a contested election for M.P.", portrays two of these racing for the polling booth. Such carriages were also turned into cabs and were called Hackney Cabs.

(Left) A private Posting Chariot, turned out with postilions and four. The horses are wearing collars and the off (right) wheeler is harnessed with a backpad from a wheel set of harness.

When a pair only is used, with one postilion up, it is called "demi-daumont." Queen Elizabeth II customarily uses such a turn-out to review troops at the annual Trooping of the Color in June.

COACHES, CARRIAGES, AND CARTS: TYPE, USE, DESIGN, AND INDUSTRY

COACHING AND THE FOUR-IN-HAND

Nostalgia for driving four spirited horses to a coach spurred the gentry into rivalries in acquiring blooded coach horses and fine coaches and carriages. Driving became a sporting endeavor, and coaching meets were held, where devotees could display their most recent purchases. Opportunities for display included going to the races, or dinner meetings, and parades in the park, where both ladies and gentlemen "took the air" in the early afternoon. Exclusive driving clubs were formed, where members set down rigid rules for types of harness, coach, livery and method of driving. No matter which pertained to turn-out was considered too trivial for wrangling at a club meeting.

A **Team** of horses was composed of four horses. The two closest to the carriage were called the wheelers, and were expected to really provide the draft (pulling power). A second pair, called the leaders, was brought into draft as needed, their main job being to carry the bars just off the pole crab. A four-in-hand team was the central unit in a coaching establishment.

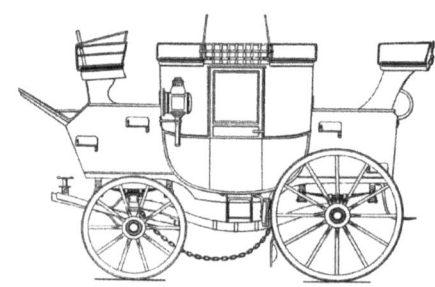

James Hazen Hyde driving the LIBERTY from New York to Lakewood in 1901.

88 COACHES, CARRIAGES, AND CARTS: TYPE, USE, DESIGN, AND INDUSTRY

Driving carriages for pleasure was a late development in the history of horse usage. Men were expected to demonstrate their ability to put a horse through the "haute ecole." When Carrousels became popular social events in the riding halls of European capitals, women began to drive themselves in these lavish spectacles, the shift to permitting a lady to drive in public was only natural. It was then that the distinctions were drawn between which carriages were suitable for a lady and which carriages were suitable for a gentleman.

E. von der Horst Koch driving Mr. Alfred G. Vanderbilt's second coach, the Viking, in England in 1910. He was considered by one enthusiast to be "the most finished Coachman I ever saw handle four reins."

When the head of the family wished to drive personally, but did not wish to use his coach and four, the wheelers were put to his privately driven carriage called a Mail Phaeton. By contrast, the leaders from the same team, which were lighter and therefore considered more suitable for a woman to drive, were put to a carriage reserved exclusively for the lady of the house. Such distinctions were rigidly maintained, and determine some of the rules for pleasure driving shows even today.

MAIL PHAETON

LADIES' DRIVING PHAETON

COACHES, CARRIAGES, AND CARTS: TYPE, USE, DESIGN, AND INDUSTRY

THE LADIES' FOUR-IN-HAND DRIVING CLUB

Driving Clubs were formed in London around 1810, one of the first and most successful being the BDC (Bedfont Driving Club), founded by Sir Henry Peyton. The Four-in-Hand Club was founded in 1856. It was limited to only thirty members at first, but membership was increased to fifty in 1886. Since there were far more "whips" than memberships, a second club was founded in 1870. The New York Coaching Club was established in 1875.

Miss Marion Hollins, whip of the public stage coach "Liberty."

All of these clubs were for "gentlemen only." They did not admit ladies to membership. In 1901, a spirited group of young ladies organized themselves into a club of their own and named it the Ladies Four-In-Hand Driving Club.

Guided by the professional coaching instructor, Morris Howlett, son of the legendary professional instructor and author, Edwin Howlett, they quickly became proficient with the ribbons, and their comings and goings were recorded in the society pages as well as sporting magazines.

One of the world's foremost women drivers today is Gloria Austin, founder of the Equine Heritage Institute. She is widely recognized for her singular accomplishments in driving singles and pairs. However, coaching and four-in-hand driving is her finest achievement. She has competed at major shows throughout the United States, Canada and in Europe. In 1999, she made a widely publicized coaching trip through England, France, Belgium and the Netherlands. She was elected to membership in the World Coaching Club in August, 1998 and is a Founding Member of the recently established Four-in-Hand Club, the first coaching club in history to admit both women and men. Fourteen four-in-hand turnouts attended its initial meet at Upperville, VA in the Spring of 2000.

The Drags of the Ladies Four-in-Hand Club are assembled on Seventy-second Street and Fifth Avenue, prior to a "parade" in Central Park.

Miss Mary Harriman is driving the Harriman family coach. She is accompanied by Mr. Thomas Hastings, Miss Cornelia Harriman, Mr. John R. Townsend, and Mr. Peter Gerry.

Mrs. C. Ledyard Blair is driving the "Liberty," the coach of James Hazen Hyde, made famous by his record run from New York to Philadelphia and back in 76 hours. Her guests are Mr. George Mifflin Wharton and Miss Georgia H. Farr.

Mrs. Ralph Sanger driving the Club Coach. She is accompanied by Mr. And Mrs. August Belmont, Jr., Mr. Sanger and Miss Wenanah Wetmore.

Mrs. W. Goodby Loew driving her coach, accompanied by her husband. Her guests include Miss Angelica Gerry, Mrs. Howard Brokaw and Mr. Worthington Whitehouse.

LIVERY

Postilions in livery

Turning out a coach required various servants, whose tasks were very defined, and whose position and rank were indicated by the uniforms they wore. Livery is the inclusive term for the various uniforms worn by coachmen, footmen, postilions and other attendants.

The two grooms are mounting in unison as the owner starts off.

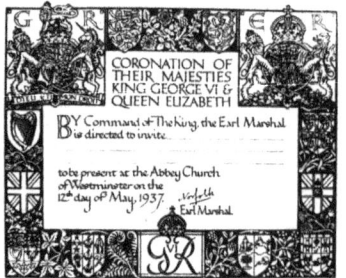

A **State Occasion** required the most formal of all livery, the use of the most ornate of carriages and the finest of harness, which had much brass or silver furniture and garnish. Here, the Irish State Coach is being readied for a State Opening of Parliament.

A Gentleman's Private Coach. Only one seat has been built on the top of such a coach to accommodate passengers, but it had only outside rails. There were no lazy-backs. Two grooms sat at the rear, on a seat supported by iron standards. This is a painting entitled: A drag with a team of well-matched strawberry roans, by C. Cooper Henderson.

92 COACHES, CARRIAGES, AND CARTS: TYPE, USE, DESIGN, AND INDUSTRY

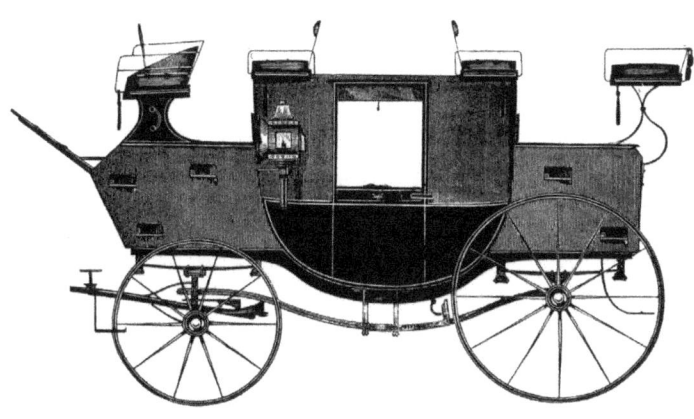

The epitome of a fine carriage was the Gentleman's Private Coach, or Drag. It developed from the English Stagecoach and the Royal Mail Coach, but was a refined, elegant vehicle, displaying the finest of craftsmanship. Although its colors were restrained and rather dark, as dictated by the Victorian conservatism, the finest of coach paints were used to attain a high mirror finish.

As successful businessmen took up pleasure driving as a suitable pastime, the sport required the use of servants for whom livery was provided. A Coachman's Dress coat was denoted by six buttons in front and four in back; the Footman's coat had five buttons in front and six in back. Each wore a top hat and had leather knee boots which had russet tops.

A TOWN COACH - a vehicle, which required a Coachman and a Groom in formal livery.

COACHES, CARRIAGES, AND CARTS: TYPE, USE, DESIGN, AND INDUSTRY

GLOSSARY

Axle - the most basic component of a carriage. It holds the wheels.

Body - part of the vehicle where the driver and passengers ride.

Brezel - a hand piece to which all reins are coupled in the Hungarian Method. Although there are several ways by which reins may be coupled to it, each rein eventually couples back to this single hand piece.

Cabriolet - a two-wheel carriage pulled by one horse and intended for the owner's private driving. Many second-hand Cabriolets were found eminently suitable for "taxi" work.

C-Spring - developed from the S-spring, which had been commonly used to hang bodies on eighteenth century vehicles. The first modification was to turn the head down, creating the Crane Neck Spring. From that, it was only a matter of time, before the spring was bent over into a C shape.

Clubbing - the procedure of placing all reins in the left hand by placing the off reins on top of the hand with the index finger separating the off reins.

Chariot - belongs to that set of carriages, which are marked by "horizontal springs placed immediately on the axles, to intercept the concussion of the wheels, and sustain the whole weight of both body and carriage; and circular upright springs, to sustain the body.

Char-A-Banc - a heavy sporting Break distinguished by multiple seats. This was a heavy vehicle and could be used for long distance driving as well as exercising the four-in-hand.

Chuck Wagon - By adding a "chuck box" at the back of the wagon box, and perhaps one at the front as well, an ordinary farm wagon converted became the "kitchen" for many a cowboy at work on the range.

Concord Coach - this vehicle was gradually acknowledged as the archetype of the American stagecoach. It was offered in three sizes, a 6 Passenger, 9 Passenger and 12 Passenger, each denoting the inside passenger capacity. Typically, they carried additional passengers on roof seats and on the roof itself.

Curricle is actually a Chaise which has been adapted for driving a pair of horses to a two-wheel vehicle. The body is heavier and more substantial, and it is usually hung from C-springs on leather thoroughbraces. Many of them have a French hood, called a **Calash.**

Curricle Bar - steel bar that hangs from the pole and mounts to the terrets that are attached to the horses.

de rigeur - a knowledge of the whips proper use. No driver is excused from the need to know how to use a whip properly.

Diligence - a multi-passenger, very large coach with several passenger compartments, both inside and outside.

Dish - a slight concave shape to the wheel. It prevents the spoke from breaking through the sidewall of the felloe when the wheel is raised up by a stone during travel, which it would do if the spokes entered at a ninety-degree angle.

Dirtboard - A guard that keeps dirt from the axle arm.
Dress Chariot - a mark of the aristocrat's coach house, a Chariot turned out formally, with liveried coachman and grooms.
Double Elbow Spring - also called the half elliptic.
Eight Spring Suspension System - Four C-springs were used together with four elliptic springs to create a superb spring suspension system.
Elliptic Spring - The combination of two half-elliptic springs produces the Elliptic spring, the most commonly used spring on most small carriages.
Fifth-Wheel - A four-wheel vehicle actually has another "wheel" assembly, which permits the front axle to turn. In some instances, when the unit has large metal rings, somewhat resembling a wheel, it allows the axle to turn. In other cases, it is composed merely of two small metal plates.
Felloes - form the rim of the wheel and are upon that rim that the wheel rides.
Forecarriage - On a four-wheeled vehicle, the forward part of the running gear.
Four-Wheel Dog - has four elliptic springs, one at each corner of the axle.
French-Platform Spring - When heavier carriage bodies needed additional support, two elbow springs were added. This created the French-Platform Spring, and it was referred to as a five-spring suspension system.
Full Hand Method - is used in France, one rein over the fore-finger and one between each successive finger.
Gear - the combination of wheels, axle, reach and springs making a mechanical cradle for the body.
Governess Cart - vehicle hung on elliptic springs and a crank axle, which allows the body to hang lower.
Hand Horse - the off horse, in postilion driving. It is "led" by a single rein, which has a small ring at the end. This ring runs on a small strap, which is attached to the sides of the bit. The post boy rode the near wheeler horse and led the off horse, guiding it with the postilion whip held in his right hand.
Half-Elliptic - is a leaf spring, which is the basic component of all other springs. The ends of the largest leaf are curled and the leaf spring is itself curled before the eye is rolled; it is said to have a Double Sweep and can help lessen excessive carriage movement.
Heraldry - the complex and historic process of determining such coats of arms, provided all sorts of allegorical and fanciful designs, for such coats of arms.
Hounds - the inside futchells of heavy wagons and stage coaches.
Hub - made of oak in England and elm in America, is the vortex around which the spokes are arranged.
Hungarian or Wilson Snaffle - with a jointed mouthpiece is an acceptable driving bit. It is the most common type of bit used. It consists of a bit mouthpiece with a ring on either side and acts with direct pressure. The snaffle bit works on several parts of the horse's mouth.

Kladruber horse - considered rare, having old Spanish and Italian blood, shares a common ancestry with the Lipizzan. It is the national horse of the Czech Republic. Greys were used as a majestic ceremonial horse by the imperial Court in Vienna while, black horses were used by high-level church officials. Their peaceful and well-balanced nature makes these animals perfect for equine-assisted therapy and an ideal team for leisure drives.

Livery - is the inclusive term for the various uniforms worn by coachmen, footmen, postilions and other attendants. Specific rules were set down for every occasion, and the each type of occasion required markedly different uniforms.

Lock - The distance the axle can turn.

Mail Axle - In 1786, John Besant patented a wheel carriage, which included a new type of axle. He created a chamber in which oil could be stored. The wheel was held on the axle by a moon plate, a metal plate surrounding the axle, using three bolts, which pierced the hub of the wheel. It was sealed with a leather washer to keep the oil from leaking out. This type of axle was extensively used on Mail Coaches.

Matinee Wagon - The four-wheel sulky with its balloon-tire form, thought by some to give greater stability, appeared almost at the same time as the two-wheel sulky.

Mitchell Wagon - was known far and wide as an excellent farm and ranch wagon.

Morgan horse - is the only breed founded by a single stallion and the only breed named for its foundation sire. Among the many uses of the Morgan horse, his natural ability to draw great weight made him an ideal driving horse.

Pace - a gait in which the horse moves two legs on the same side. The pace is considered faster than the trot by 4 or 5 seconds.

Park Harness - deemed more appropriate for a team pulling a Gentleman's Private Coach, or Drag. It was more elegant, and refined and showed more patent leather. It is especially marked by the use of russet collars, and sometimes the addition of loin straos and trace carriers.

Pole - piece that comes from the pivoting front axle of the carriage, between the horses to the front, and attaches to pole strap on the horses. The pole allows the horses to stop the carriage without the carriage bumping into the back of the horses.

Poll pressure - mouth pressure, or chin pressure. Pressure is exerted on the poll (top of the head of horse) by using the mouthpiece as a fulcrum to pull on the cheek straps and headband.

Port - a mouthpiece that accommodates the horse's tongue, when a straight bar mouthpiece proves unaccommodating to the horse.

Posting - the system of using postilions (riders) to drive horses rented at inns and livery stables along a route. One postilion, who was in charge of the turn-out, rode the near (left) wheeler; a second postilion rode the near leader.

Platform Spring - which is two half-elliptic springs perpendicular to the axle and two half-elliptic springs parallel to it. Such a form of springing was also called a Telegraph Spring or a Mail Spring since such springs as these were used on Mail Coaches.

Ride Horse - the near wheeler horse, on which the postilion rider is mounted.

Roof-Seat Break - a natural progression from the Wagonette Break, since no one really wanted to ride in the body any more. That was now only for the storage of horse blankets, driving rugs, headstalls and rain gear.

Road Cart - a dual purpose vehicle, used for exercise or for making fast trips to town, since the frugal American farmer was reluctant to buy a sulky/skeleton cart, which could only be used for racing.

Road Coach harness - was somewhat more coarse, having been developed from the utilitarian harness of Mail Coach days.

Skeleton Break or Break - the vehicle properly used for training teams of horses and to exercise them. There was a platform behind the driver's seat for helpers to ride and easily dismount. Sometimes, the weight of the vehicle was increased by adding a wooden box, filled with lead, to the back axle.

Snaffle Position - for the rein (which is just a direct pull.)

Sociable - the American public "Sociable" was for public use and had windows and a rack for luggage and parcels on its roof. It was suspended on cee springs.

Spokes of a Wheel - do not enter the hub or the felloe at a straight angle. They enter at a slight angle, sometimes no more than one-eighth of an inch.

State Occasion - required the most formal of all livery, the use of the most ornate of carriages and the finest of harness, which had much brass or silver furniture and garnish.

Stanhope Gig - marked especially by the use of the Platform Spring, which is two half-elliptic springs perpendicular to the axle and two half-elliptic springs parallel to it.

Steel Axle - consists of a steel bar, whose ends have been fashioned into a spindle. The end is turned further down and threaded to accommodate a nut. A collar is fitted behind the spindle to stop the wheel from going further. A metal boxing was fitted inside the wooden hub of the wheel, which permitted the wheel to rotate.

Studebaker Dump Cart - The earliest vehicles had only two wheels. The body was placed upon an axle without any benefit of springing.

Sulky - was developed as a lightweight vehicle to barely carry a driver. It is often referred to as a skeleton cart.

Swales Bit - is a unique driving bit, which exerts no poll pressure.

Tandem Cart - a form of the Dog Cart, only its body is set higher and is more substantial.

Tandem driving - driving one horse in front of another.

Team - a group of horses pulling a vehicle composed of four horses. The two closest to the carriage were called the wheelers, and were expected to really provide the draft (pulling power). A second pair, called the leaders, was brought into draft as needed, their main job being to carry the bars just off the pole crab.

Telegraph Spring - is a combination of two half elliptic springs, sweeping up, and two half-elliptic springs, sweeping down. The four springs are attached together with a shackle. Since the springs created a sort of platform, it was also called a Platform Spring and, since it was commonly used on the Mail Coach, it was also called the Mail Spring.

Terret - the steel rollers on which the curricle bar rode. It was mounted at the center of the packpad of the harness.

Troika - a Russian vehicle in which there is only an outside rein to the galloping horses, a check rein being used to hook them to the trotting horse in the center. The driver holds his arms outstretched in front of himself.

The Whip - The driver carried a whip, which became the singular badge of the "coachman." The driver became fashionably known as the "The Whip."

Three-Spring Platform Spring - When one of the elliptic springs were removed from the Platform Spring, and the ends of the half-elliptics were attached to the body of the carriage by a metal bracket. It is also known as the Dennet Spring.

Tiger - A dickey seat at the rear is provided for a groom, a diminutive servant.

Tilbury Spring - also known as the Gallows Spring, is a combination of three springs. An elliptic spring, with a double sweep, is hung on a metal bracket, ignominiously called a "gallows bracket." Two elbow springs are then attached to each eye, and to the body of the carriage.

Trot - a gait in which the horse moves two legs on opposite sides. It is the gait of the Carriage Horse because it is the most sustainable gait over a long distance.

Village Cart - Village Cart has three springs, two half-elliptic springs mounted perpendicular to the axle, the front of which are attached to the shafts. At the back is a half-elliptic spring with a double sweep.

Wagonette Break - one of the preeminent forms of exercise vehicle. With a second seat is also called a Built-up Break or a Body Break.

Wheelwright - a person who makes or repairs wooden wheels.